C000212683

# GOOGLE ADVERTISING GUERRILLA TACTICS

## GOOGLE ADVERTISING A-Z PLUS 150 KILLER ADWORDS TIPS & TRICKS

# GOOGLE ADVERTISING GUERRILLA TACTICS
## GOOGLE ADVERTISING A-Z PLUS 150 KILLER ADWORDS TIPS & TRICKS

First Edition
Manufactured in the United States and/or the United Kingdom
10 9 8 7 6 5 4 3 2 1
ISBN: 978-1-933747-01-9

BottleTreeBooks.com

**Copyrights:** BottleTree Logo and *Google Advertising Guerrilla Tactics: Google Advertising A-Z Plus 150 Killer AdWords Tips & Tricks* are Copyrights © of BottleTree Books, LLC. All Rights Reserved. No part of this work may be reproduced, stored in a retrieval system or transmitted in any media.

**Trademarks:** BOTTLETREE, BOTTLETREE BOOKS, GOOGLE ADVERTISING GUERILLA TACTICS, BOTTLETREEBOOKS.COM, BottleTree Logo, and related trade dress, including all cover art designs are trademarks of BottleTree Books, LLC, and may not be used without written permission. Google is a trademark of Google Technology Inc. All other trademarks are the intellectual property of their respective owners. BottleTree Books LLC is not associated with Google Technology Inc. (but loves everything Google!) or any other company cited herein.

**Limitation of Liability & Disclaimer of Warranty:** BOTTLETREE BOOKS LLC AND THE AUTHOR(S) MAKE NO REPRESENTATIONS OF WARRANTY WITH RESPECT TO THE ACCURACY OR COMPLETENESS OF THE CONTENTS OF THIS WORK AND SPECIFICALLY DISCLAIM ALL WARRANTIES, INCLUDING THE WARRANTIES OF MERCHANTABILITY AND FITNESS FOR A PARTICULAR PURPOSE. NO WARRANTY MAY BE CREATED OR EXTENDED BY SALES, WEBSITE ADVERTISING OR PROMOTIONAL MATERIALS. THE ADVICE AND STRATEGIES CONTAINED IN THIS WORK MAY NOT BE SUITABLE FOR ALL SITUATIONS. NOTHING IN THIS WORK IS TO BE CONSTRUED AS ACCOUNTING ADVICE, LEGAL ADVICE OR COUNSELING, OR OTHER PROFESSIONAL SERVICES. NEITHER BOTTLETREE BOOKS LLC NOR THE AUTHOR(S) WILL BE LIABLE FOR ANY DAMAGES ARISING FROM THE ADVICE AND STRATEGIES IN THIS WORK. THE LISTING OF AN ORGANIZATION, WEBSITE, OR URL IN THIS WORK DOES NOT NECESSARILY MEAN THAT BOTTLETREE BOOKS LLC OR THE AUTHOR(S) ENDORSES INFORMATION FROM SUCH ORGANIZATION, WEBSITE OR THAT CONTAINED AT THE URL OR RECOMMENDATIONS IT MAY EMPLOY. MOREOVER, INFORMATION FROM THE LISTED ORGANIZATION, WEBSITE, OR URL MAY HAVE CHANGED SINCE PUBLICATION OF THIS WORK.

## TABLE OF CONTENTS

## I.    Introduction

### A. Huge Business Potential of Google Advertising

Google is one of the most widely used search engines. Neilsen/Net Ratings recently disclosed that Google accounts for over 45% of all US Internet searches. Google states that its network reaches 80% of all Internet users. It gains 60 million unique viewers per month with over 200 million searches conducted every day. This results in over 8 million searches per hour, 140 thousand searches each minute or over 2000 searches every *second* by people and businesses hungry to buy your products and services. Google is also one of the most comprehensive search engines. It reviews over 8 billion Websites for each query to return the most relevant results. Google does not limit itself to the Web. It also promotes advertisers by showing certain ads in traditional print magazines. The potential to increase your business using Google advertising is huge.

### 1. Self-Service Sign-Up

Signing up at www.AdWords.Google.com is easy and it takes only a few minutes. Once your credit or debit card information has been inputted, your Ad Groups created, and your ads approved for listing, they begin showing almost immediately. This can all be done online with no sign-up fees.

### 2. Jumpstart Sign-Up

If you want Google specialists to craft your campaign from the start, Google's Jumpstart program may be for you. Please visit www.adwords.google.com/select/jumpstartwelcome to get started.

### NEW ADVERTISERS ONLY

Google's Jumpstart program is only available to new U.S. advertisers that are targeting English language customers.

If you are willing to spend at least $30 per day and $299 for the sign-up fee, the Jumpstart program is a great opportunity to let the experts fine-tune your ads from the start.

### SIGN-UP FEE APPLIED TO AD CLICKS

> Your $299 Jumpstart sign-up fee will not be wasted. Google applies it as credit toward your initial AdWords clicks.

After receiving your business and advertising data, a Google specialist will contact you within 2-5 business days. Below is a comparison of the two sign-up options available to you on Google.

| Options | Jumpstart | Self-Service |
|---|---|---|
| Method | Online | Online |
| Cost | $299 USD | Free |
| Ad Up & Running | 2-5 Business Days | Immediately |
| Min. Spend | $30/Month | None |
| Keyword Selection Assistance | Yes | No |
| Budget Management Assistance | Yes | No |
| Ad Title Assistance | Yes | No |
| Ad Description Assistance | Yes | No |
| Ad URL Link Assistance | Yes | No |
| Tailored Proposal | Yes | No |

| How to Contact Google |
|:---:|
| Google Inc.<br>1600 Amphitheatre Parkway<br>Mountain View, CA 94043<br>USA<br><br>Tel: +1 (650) 253 0000<br>Fax: +1 (650) 618 1499 |

If you expect to spend at least $4000 USD/month on advertising, Google will assign an AdWords specialist to craft your ads. If this is the case, you can fill out a Google online form http://services.google.com/ads_inquiry/en to get started.

## NO GUARANTEE OF GETTING INTO THE "BLUE"

Being a Premium Sponsor with Google used to guarantee placement across the top of the search results in the "blue" area. Not any more. Your must be a top performer on Google to get placement in this coveted area (i.e., you must have a great Click-Through-Rate and high Cost-Per-Click)

### 3. Free AdWords Coupons & Merchant Solutions

Merchant Solutions is a Yahoo dedicated ecommerce solution for businesses of all sizes. It handles all aspects of ecommerce selling in one central location. Under this one-stop shop for your online products you can use Store Manager to update products listings and information without having to upload this information by a separate feed. Why are we discussing the program in a book about Google? Because by signing up you can get free Google advertising coupons. Here are the three options for Merchant Solutions programs. Note how the monthly price increases with each but the cost per transaction goes down.

| Programs | Price/Month USD | Transaction Fees | Setup Fees | Key Features |
|---|---|---|---|---|
| Starter | $39.95 | 1.5% | $50 | E-Commerce Site w/Shopping Cart, 24 Hour Support, UPS Tracking |
| Standard | $99.95 | 1.0% | $50 | Starter Features + Gift Certificates & Coupons |
| Professional | $299.95 | 0.75% | $50 | Standard + More Website, Email & Sub-Domain Name Capacity |

**JOIN BEFORE SIGNING UP FOR GOOGLE ADVERTISING**

With each Merchant Solution program you will receive $50 click credit on *both* Yahoo and Google. If you are going to register with Merchant Solutions, do it *before* signing up for Yahoo or Google advertising to get these free click credits.

To sign up for Merchant Solutions, simply call 1-866-781-9246 or visit http://smallbusiness.yahoo.com/merchant.

## B. Introduction to AdWords

The advertising opportunities are limitless and Google has developed two revolutionary ways in which you can tap these search results. For Web advertisers the program is called AdWords and for Web publishers the program is called AdSense. We will explore each of these programs in detail and provide great tips and tricks for getting the most clicks no matter which program you use.

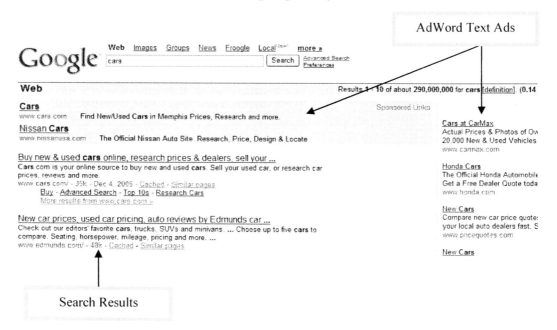

AdWord Text Ads

Search Results

## 1. Best Spot on the Search Results Page

The most coveted space on Google's search results page is the top AdWords ad in the blue rectangle. These blue area ads are two lines consisting of a Title on the first line and the URL and ad text on the second line. It has been shown that users scan from top to bottom and left to right first, paying little attention to the most relevant results and instead reading the *first* results they come across. We will show you how to get your ads in this coveted blue area later on.

## 2. Second Best Spot on the Search Results Page

The second best spot within Google's search results page is the first Website search result under the blue rectangle. You get listed here by having the most relevant and popular Website for the particular search term.

## 3. Third Best Spot on the Search Results Page

The third most coveted space is in the right-hand column next to Google's search results where the AdWords column is displayed – four lines of text that identify your business, products, or services and provide a link to your Website. Image Ads are graphic ads that are shown in place of AdWords text ads on Google partner sites. When users type in one of your designated search terms or "keywords," impressions of your ad are shown. You can choose to pay on a Cost-Per-Click (CPC) basis, which means you only pay when your ad is clicked on, or you may also run ads where you pay on a Cost-Per-Impression (CPM) basis instead of per click. Under the pay-per-click option, you get free advertising unless someone clicks on your ad, while under the Cost-Per-Impression model you get free clicks no matter how many times your ad is clicked on, but you pay for advertising even you don't receive any clicks.

| | |
|---|---|
| **Title Line:** | Entire Tales & Poems of Poe |
| **Bodyline1:** | Photographic & Annotated Edition of |
| **Bodyline2:** | World's Most Haunting & Mysterious Author. |
| **URL Line:** | AndrewBarger.com |

**Image Ad**

AdWords and Image Ads are displayed in any Internet Explorer or Netscape browser higher than version 2.X, which means 99% of Internet users will be able to see your ad. This also includes Apple's popular Safari browser and FireFox.

## NO IMAGE ADS ON THE GOOGLE SEARCH RESULTS PAGE

Currently Google only allows AdWords text ads on its popular search results pages.

Before you get started, Google provides free data on 13 major business categories in its "For Your Industry" section within the AdWords Help Center https://adwords.google.com/support/?hl=en_US under AdWords Resources.

| Google Data on 13 Business Categories |
|---|
| 1. Automotive |
| 2. Business & Industrial Markets |

3. Consumer Packaged Goods
4. Entertainment
5. Financial Services
6. Gaming
7. Healthcare
8. Real Estate
9. Retail
10. Tech B2B
11. Technology Commerce
12. Telecom
13. Travel

Below you'll learn how to get top placement with AdWords and Image Ads by paying a fraction of what your competitors do. You'll also learn how to make your ads stand out among the rest even if you don't get top placement. The AdSense program will be reviewed in detail so that you'll learn how generate the most revenue by placing AdWords and Image Ads on your Website. In addition, you'll discover how to launch an effective advertising campaign on Google that is finely tuned to the best keywords, which will get you not only the most click-throughs, but also the most sales. We'll demonstrate which ads work the best in primary market areas. Along the way you'll be shown essential tips and tricks for getting the most clicks and increasing sales. Using *Guerrilla Google Advertising* you'll be on your way to increased profitability at the lowest cost to leapfrog you over the competition. So let's get started.

### C. Vast Reach of Google Advertising

Google has compiled two networks on which AdWords and Image Ads are displayed. These are broken down into the Search and Content Networks. For the purposes of this book, we have divided them even further to include the Google Internal Network of search pages. Millions of individual Websites also display ads on the

AdSense Network. Here is a snapshot of each.

### 1. Search Network

Let's first consider the powerful Google Search Network. After all, search is how Google rose to Internet stardom. On the Search Network AdWords text ads and Image Ads are shown above, below and to the right-hand side of search results. Impressions are triggered by linking of the search terms to keywords bid on by AdWords advertisers.

### a. Internal Search Network

Google has launched a myriad of great internal services where your ads will be displayed.

Here is a list of potential Google Internal Network sites that may become available to show ads in the future:

### b. External Search Network

Google has used its innovative technology to partner with some of the Internet's most widely used search engines and portals such as AOL, CompuServe, Ask Jeeves, etc. Not only are AdWords displayed each time one of the 200 million searches are conducted each day on Google, they are also displayed during searches on Google's partner sites.

## LACK OF CONTROL ON THE SEARCH NETWORK

Currently, you are unable to select which partners show your ads in the Google Search Network.

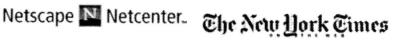
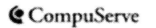

## WILL THE AOL ADVERTISING DEAL AFFECT YOUR CAMPAIGN?

In 2005 Google signed a much-publicized advertising deal with AOL. Under the deal AOL will receive a credit for advertising clicks on Google. This will not, however, affect your campaign as the highest quality ads will still get top position. It will, however, allow AOL to increase its maximum CPC to get the top position since it will be receiving a discount.

## 2. Content Network

Google has also compiled an impressive array of Websites on which AdWords and Image Ads are displayed when users search on specific articles. Google's Content Network reaches over 64% of unique Internet users (Source: ComScore's machine-based panel), spanning over 100 and 20 different languages. Initially the Content Network consisted of news Websites, but quickly grew into much more.

## CONTROL ON THE CONTENT NETWORK

> Unlike the Google Search Network, you are in control of which partners show your ads on the Google Content Network.

### a. Internal Content Network

The Google Internal Content Network consists of Websites on which AdSense publishers display AdWords ads. It also consists of a few Google properties where ads are displayed alongside content.

But is the vast AdSense network that includes tens of thousands of Websites where impressions of your ads may be shown. AdSense allows your AdWords and Image Ads to be displayed on the billions of individual Website pages that exist on the Internet. Google searches the enabled Websites and inserts AdWords or Image Ads that would be tailored to the interests of visitors. When the ads are clicked on, Google pays the Website owner a percentage of the amount paid to Google, i.e., the CPC, just as it does for book publishers with Google Book Search. Here is a sample horizontal AdSense ad unit of ads that would appear on a Webpage:

**Leaderboard (728 x 90)**

| Free Telescope Catalog | Celestron Telescope | SkyOptics.com | Telescope Eyepieces |
|---|---|---|---|
| Low prices on dozens of telescopes at Orion's web site. | Minimum prices for Auth, USA Dealer BizRate "Best of the Best" Shop Now | Binoculars, night vision, tripods, rangefinders and telescopes. | A large variety including eyepieces for astrophotography! MaxView |
| | | | Ads by Google |

### "I'M FEELING LUCKY" BUTTON

The "I'm Feeling Luck" button will not trigger ads unless they are shown via AdSense. The button takes Internet users directly to the Web page that Google believes is most appropriate for the inputted search term. Unless that Web page is enabled with AdSense ads, none are shown.

## Amazon.com

The Internal Content Network includes Websites with a single page to vast merchant sites like Amazon.com, which all run AdSense ads.

### b. External Content Network

The External Content Network shows AdWords ads placed adjacent various articles and news related items. This includes some of the Web's top information properties and traditional print media such as magazines.

Below is a selection of some of the Web properties where AdWords ads are displayed.

Following is a list of magazines where ads have begun appearing.

| Automotive | Lifestyle | Technology |
|---|---|---|
| Car and Driver | Budget Living | Computer Shopping |
| Cycle World | Dwell | Computerworld |
| Import Tuner | Ellegirl | CRN |
| Motor Trend | Entrepreneur | Information Week |
| Road and Track | Home | InfoWorld |
| Sport Compact Car | Martha Stewart Kids | MacAddict |
| | Martha Stewart Living | Network Computing |
| | Outdoor Photographer | PC Magazine |
| | Pregnancy | PC Photo |
| | Women's Health | PC World |
| | Women's Health & Fitness | OXM |

Google's auction process for magazines is simple. When it is about to launch a new print advertising campaign, Google sends out an email to AdWords advertisers who log in, select the magazine(s) in which they want to advertise, input the maximum they are willing to bid for full, &frac12, and &frac 14 page ad units. A deadline for submission of bids is given and Google notifies the winning bidders who are then given a second deadline in which to submit ad copy for display in the magazine.

### D. Google Advertising Structure

Google has broken down its advertising structure into two main parts: Campaigns, and Ad Groups. Beneath these you specify the keywords applicable to each, the countries in which the ad will run, and the languages in which the ad will be displayed.

**Google Advertising Structure**

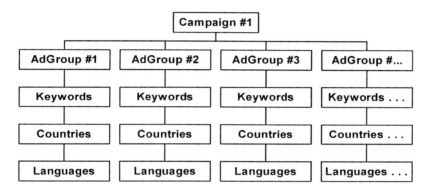

### 1. Campaigns

The first level in Google's advertising structure is the Campaign level. Think of this level as a product category for your marketing strategy.

#### USE THE AD OPTIMIZATION BUTTON

The Campaign Summary page includes a check box for ad optimization. By ensuring this box is checked, Google will issue more impressions of your ad for keywords that are getting the most clicks. Likewise, it will slow impressions for keywords not receiving many clicks.

If you have an online store that sells shirts, shoes, hats and scarves, a

Campaign should be started for each of these categories.

## KEYWORDS FOR SEPARATE CAMPAIGNS

> You can create the same list of keywords in separate Campaigns, but Google will only show 1 ad per account for a keyword search. By doing this, your ads will not dominate the AdWords column, but rather will compete against each other.

## 2. Ad Groups

Numerous Ad Groups can be created in each Campaign. In our example above, under the shirts campaign, separate Ad Groups could be created for "dress shirts," "long sleeve shirts," "flannel shirts," etc. within a "shirts" Campaign.

### Limits on Google's Advertising Structure

1. 25 Maximum Campaigns Per Account
2. 100 Maximum Ad Groups Per Campaign
3. 10,000 Maximum Keywords Per Ad Group

This means you have 25 million variations to determine which keywords are generating the most click-throughs for your ads!

Ads shown for each Ad Group are rotated evenly. Google tracks which are performing the best by having the greatest CTR and highest CPC. You can then remove your poorly performing ads or tweak them for optimum CTRs. We'll discuss Quality Scores later.

## CREATE AN AD GROUP FOR EACH KEYWORD

If you are marketing a few specific products or services, and bidding on a handful of highly specific keywords, create an Ad Group for *each* keyword or phrase that uses that keyword or phrase in the Title. Imagine the interest your ad will draw if when users type in "Yahoo Advertising" they get the following:

**Yahoo Advertising A-Z**
Plus 110 Tips & Tricks for
Getting the Most Clicks!
BottleTreeBooks.com

## E. Low Google Advertising Costs

Now that the vast scope and reach of Google advertising have been established, let's cut right to the chase: How much will you pay to reach this kind of audience: $100, $1000, $10,000? How about $0.01? For as little as $0.01 per click (if you have a high click through rate) and $0.01 per day you can advertise on Google. You set the amount you are willing to spend on advertising. Once customers click on your ad and have used up your max daily budget, your ad will no longer run for that day unless you instruct Google otherwise. You can place separate bids for the Search and Content Networks.

## YIN AND YANG OF THE BUDGET OPTIMIZER

Apart from the manual way, Google let's you set your daily spending, its Budget Optimizer tool will automatically adjust the CPC to maximize your clicks. Be warned, Google will ensure that you spend your daily budget so set it at a reasonable level.

You are always in control of your advertising budget and the cost barriers are nonexistent to advertise on Google.

| Minimum Cost-Per-Click | Maximum Cost-Per-Click |
| --- | --- |
| $0.01 USD | $100 USD |

## SMART PRICING WORKS FOR YOU

Google has built-in Smart Pricing that adjusts your CPC lower on the Content Network if clicks are not getting "business results." It includes revenues, email list registrations, clicks on AdSense advertisements that may be displayed on your Website, newsletter signups, etc.

The amount you pay each day can also be as little as $0.01 up to an unlimited amount and you can specify one bid amount for a particular ad on the Search Network and another on the Content Network. There are no monthly commitments or minimum monthly expenditures for your advertisements on Google and it only charges a $5 sign up fee.

| Minimum Daily Budget | Maximum Daily Budget |
| --- | --- |
| $.01 USD | Unlimited |

## 1. How to Set Bids on the Search Network

Clicks on the Search Network are typically worth more to you as an advertiser since there is not as much "content" information on the Search Network. Searchers know what they are looking for on the Search Network and their clicks are more likely to result in sales for you. This being said, the maximum CPC is usually much higher on the Search Network than on the Content Network (usually double or more). You easily set up your Search Network max bid amounts when creating a new Campaign or an Ad Group within a Campaign. You will have two decisions: How much you want to set for your maximum CPC for each keyword and whether you want manually bidding on each keyword or to set a uniform max CPC for each keyword within your Ad Group.

## 2. How to Set Bids on the Content Network

In 2005 Google began allowing AdWords advertisers to set their own maximum bid on the Content Network that is wholly separate from what they are bidding on the Search Network. This means, in the vast majority of instances, AdWords advertisers will be paying much less for clicks on the Content Network, which includes AdSense clicks. Google makes it a bit challenging to find this option. Here is how to set this separate bid amount on the Content Network. And remember, you can place a maximum bid as low as $0.01!

---

### Set Search Network Bid Amounts

➢ Select "Edit Campaign Settings"
➢ Select "Content Network" and "Content Bids"
➢ Save these settings
➢ Return to Ad Group and Select "Edit" for "Content Bids"

---

| Campaign Management | Reports | Analytics | My Account |

Campaign Summary | Tools | Conversion Tracking

Campaign Summary > Campaign #2

**Campaign: Campaign #2** - Active | Pause Campaign | Delete Campaign
Campaign Daily Budget: USD $5.00 | Edit Campaign Settings
No campaign negative keywords. Add | No excluded sites. Add

Show all Ad Groups

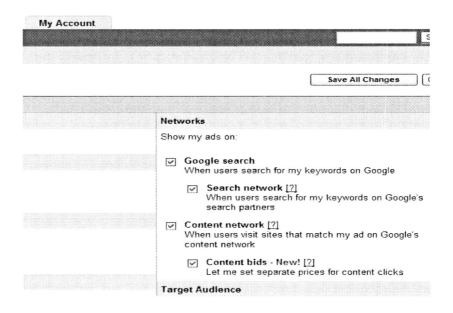

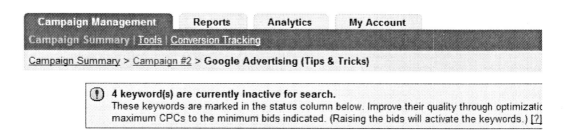

## F. Build Brand Identity for Free on Google

There are no costs for people viewing your ad on Google if you pick a Cost-Per-Click option instead of a Cost-Per-Impression model! This is a great way to build brand identity on the Internet, which is the second highest goal of marketers right behind increased sales. You will be hard pressed to find this feature on any traditional marketing medium where advertising costs are based on the number of people hearing the ad (radio) or viewing the ad (TV, billboards, magazines). With Google AdWords the traditional scattershot approach to advertising is over. You can target your ad to the exact customers needing your product or services and they actually come to you by searching for your products or services. This is direct-response advertising at its highest level. Google only requires at least 1 click per 1000 impressions of your ad. This is not much and it means that 999 potential customers could be viewing your ad free of charge. If we extrapolate the numbers, only 10 clicks are needed for 10,000 impressions, giving you 9,990 free advertisements at a minimum cost of $.10 USD given $.01 USD per click. Below we'll take a look at various bid strategies to get you top position placement.

### G. Click-to-Call

Google's Click-to-Call feature displays a small telephone symbol next to AdWord ads that are enabled with advertiser phone contact. With this innovative feature, potential customers can speak to you over the phone via the Internet. Here's how it works.

In essence, the Click-to-Call feature acts like a callback telephone service. Potential customers click on the phone symbol and then they must enter their phone number for you, the AdWords advertiser, to call them right back. Google's software calls the potential customer's number. When they pick up the phone, they hear a ringing sound as Google connects then to the advertiser.

### LIMITED CUSTOMER INFORMATION PROVIDED

Google sends the advertiser's phone number as a caller ID code so that customers can dial in the future. It does not provide customer name or address. The phone number is also blocked.

## II. Bid Strategies, Impression Frequency and Position Placement

### A. Two Ad Statuses

Monitoring which keywords are resulting in the most clicks is fundamental to having a highly effective marketing campaign. Google once again makes this easy by providing a status column for each keyword within an Ad Group.

| Two Ad Statuses |
|---|
| 1. Active; |
| 2. Inactive. |

Gone are the former, and often confusing, statuses of Normal, In Trial, On Hold, Trial-Slowed, and Disabled. Accounts are neither slowed nor new keywords disabled under the current system.

### 1. Active Status

This is the status you must achieve to be in the AdWords game. Each keyword linked to your ads now has a Quality Score. Active status is based on your Quality Score and the maximum amount you are bidding per click. This is Google advertising. Therefore, mathematical formulas are involved on which its software algorithms are modeled to automatically manage advertising accounts. With this in mind, let's breakdown the factors that make up the Quality Score.

### a. Breaking Down the Quality Score

The Quality Score is a product of the current keyword Click-Through-Rate, historical keyword performance, applicability of the keyword to the ad, content and layout of the landing page, and "other relevancy" factors.

The *Click-Through-Rate* (CTR) is easy. It is a known ratio based upon the amount of times your ad is clicked on per the number of impressions.

## NO INACTIVE STATUS FOR THE CONTENT NETWORK

> No matter how low your maximum CPC is on the Search Network or if your ads on the Search Network have fallen into "Inactive Status," your ads will keep showing on the Content Network as long as you have Content Network advertising enabled.

The minimum CTR you need to keep your ads running on Google's Search Network has dropped from 0.5% to only 0.1% as long as you bid high enough for each click.

| Minimum CTR | Maximum CTR |
|:---:|:---:|
| 0.1% | 100% |

*Historical keyword performance* (HKP) is based on a CTR over the life of the keyword you are bidding on versus over the short term, such as the last 1000 impressions. Your Quality Score has a baggage factor! That is why it's important to create relevant, compelling ads from the start.

*Relevance of the keywords to the ad* (RKA) sounds cryptic at first, but is also easy to figure out. In particular, the more keywords you use in the ad, the higher its relevance. Another key to having good relevancy of keywords is placement within the ad. For example, you should start the Title of the ad with your keyword if possible. Please see the keyword tips and tricks below for great ways to accomplish this.

*Content and layout of the landing page* (CLP) also makes up a factor of the Quality Score. Google is seeking to increase the experience of its users by providing landing pages for them that are rich in content.

This means that if your landing page is sparse, your quality score may go down and you will have to pay more for Adword clicks. Now, simply showing a product on a page with only a price and no description or reviews will hurt your Quality Score.

The *other relevancy factors* (ORF) of your Quality Score are ambiguous and not published by Google. Here are our thoughts regarding the possibilities. Google likes advertisers that spend a lot of money every month. Advertisers could be assigned an ORF number based upon their average monthly spending (short term spending). The total amount of advertising money spent with Google over the entire advertiser's history could also be assigned a value (long term spending). What's more, keywords are viewed by Google across each advertiser's *entire* account. Keywords getting few clicks can affect the Quality Score of even your best keyword ads.

## REVIEW AD GROUPS OFTEN FOR POOR KEYWORDS

> Review your keywords on a regular basis and cull those that are not performing well. They have an effect on the Quality Score for all your keywords.

Websites on the vast Content Network, which includes AdSense sites, are grouped by *themes*. For instance, one theme might be coffee bean grinder Websites. In turn, Google clusters keywords within each Ad Group and matches them with like themes within the Content Network. Each Ad Group should contain only keywords that are closely related to each other in theme. For this example, you would want to include various keywords relating to different types of coffee bean grinders, but *not* cappuccino machines or French presses. Open a new Ad Group for coffee making products.

## b. Quality Score Formula

It is likely also that Google weights each of the components of the Quality Score differently such that the CTR could be assigned a higher value than the rest. In fact, considering the formula below, the value of the numbers is likely weighted from left to right (i.e., CTR is the biggest number, HKP is the next largest, RKA the next biggest and the ORF the smallest). If QS is assigned a maximum value of 100, we estimate that CTR=40; HKP=30; RKA=15; CLP=10; ORF=5.

$$QS = CTR+HKP+RKA+CLP+ORF$$

Below we will show you how to increase each of these components to maximize your Quality Score.

## 2. Inactive Status

Inactive status is the death knell for your keywords. Ads for these keywords will no longer show impressions.

## a. Inactive Status on Search Network

Your ads remain Active based on your Quality Score and the amount you are bidding per click. When your maximum CPC falls below the minimum CPC threshold, your keyword(s) will also fall into Inactive Status. Your CTR is vital to the success of your marketing campaign on Google, but your CPC is also very important. If your maximum bid does not meet the minimum bid, your particular keyword will not trigger ads on the Search Network. Once you have increased your bid to meet that amount, you are in the game and your ads linked to that keyword will show. If either is too low, your ads will fall into Inactive status.

| How to Escape Inactive Status |
| --- |
| ➢ Improve your Quality Score using the tips provided above;<br>➢ Increase the maximum CPC;<br>➢ Delete the inactive keyword;<br>➢ Delete the inactive keyword and place it in another Ad Group;<br>➢ Let the keyword remain inactive and hope the minimum CPC falls below the maximum CPC you are willing to pay; |

## b. Inactive Status on Content Network

As stated above, no matter how low your maximum CPC is on the Search Network, your ads will keep showing on the Content Network. Why? Google is looking for inventory on its Content Network due to low CTRs. What this means for you is that you can advertise for as little as $0.01 per click on the Content Network! This includes popular Websites and site/segment targeting within those sites. You will still be competing for top position with other ads (i.e., Quality Score is still important on the Content Network), but if you can find little used keywords that have applicability to your market, you can get clicks for as little as $0.01.

| Minimum CPC | Maximum CPC |
| --- | --- |
| $0.01 | Unlimited |

Just because the minimum CPC is $0.01 does not mean you should run only your worst ads on the Content Network. In fact, it is just the opposite. You should run your *best* performing ads on the Content Network. These are the ones with the highest Quality Score and you could be getting clicks for only $0.01 each.

## B. How to Rank #1 in AdWords

At first glance Google's pay-for-performance system appears to reward those bidding the highest amount with top placement in AdWords. The logic follows that if one advertiser is paying $10 each time a customer searches on "cars" and clicks on its ad, while the next highest bidder is paying $2.50, the higher advertiser should receive top placement. Surprisingly, this is not the case! The number of *clicks* your ad receives on Google is the most important factor to gaining top placement! We will show you below tips and tricks to not only get top placement in the AdWords column, but also in the "blue" area at the top of the Google Search Network.

Ad Rank is the term used to describe ad placement within AdWords. Google determines it by multiplying the Quality Score by your maximum CPC. This simple mathematical formula is how placement is calculated:

$$\textbf{Ad Rank} = \textbf{(QS)(Max. CPC)}$$

As shown above, the Quality Score equals:

$$\textbf{QS} = \textbf{CTR+HKP+RKA+CLP+ORF}$$

What does this mean for you? There are two ways to getting a high Ad Rank on Google.

### 1. Optimization Method

The higher your Quality Score, the lower your actual CPC no matter how much you maximum CPC is. This is the smart advertiser's formula to driving more clicks at less CPC. For the smart advertiser, quality remains your best tool to a lower CPC and higher Ad Ranking on AdWords. Since we've learned that the CTR is the key component of your Quality Score, then it follows that when the number of clicks increase, so will your status in the AdWords column. Because of a high CTR, these are the ads that are making Google the most money. The amount of users clicking on your ad is more vital to your AdWords placement or rank than the amount you pay Google per click. In sum, Google wants popular ads and it will reward accordingly.

## NOTHING TO LOSE ON THE CONTENT NETWORK

The minimum bid posted for your keywords is calculated based upon advertising across all Google properties. Since your clicks (or lack thereof) on the Content Network do not affect your CTR, there is no risk to advertising on the Content Network. In fact, Google's smart pricing tool will automatically reduce your minimum CPC if an ad on the Content Network is less likely to produce results.

In limited circumstances you may be competing with ads placed by Google for its *own* products. Does Google always reserve for itself the top spot? In the test we conducted the answer is NO. A Google advertisement for AdWords was ranked second. Google's ads appear to be under the same rules as all other ads. They must have high CTRs to rank first.

If you have a CPC of $50 but you only get one click-through per week, an ad with a CPC of $1 getting 51 click-throughs will rank above you. A competitor that is only paying $1 each time a user visits its Website will be placed higher in the Google ranking system than a company paying $50 for each click! Therefore, the greater the number of clicks on your ads the less you have to pay for new business and the higher you will rank in the AdWords column.

Getting sales or opt-ins to your newsletter, etc is a two-step process. Having a high CTR on Google is only the first step. Once customers have reached your Website you must complete the sale. This cannot be stressed enough. If you have the world's best marketing campaign, but a terrible Website, you will not gain sales or opt-ins.

## 2. Brute Strength Method

The alternate way of looking at the AdRank formula is the brute strength method. If you have a lot of cash to spend on each click, your Quality Score can be lower. In fact, you can stop reading this book right now. Just throw cash at this issue, have a huge maximum CPC, and spend your way to a top ad ranking, knowing that the smart advertisers may be paying 50% or less per click than what you are paying on your ads. Likewise, they will have a much higher ROI.

## C. Physical Advertising Space on Google is Important

Only two ads are displayed in the blue rectangle above Google's search results. The number of Google ads visible in the AdWords column without scrolling is only seven with an Internet Explorer browser on "full screen" view. Google displays a maximum of eight in the AdWords column, but users must scroll down to the see the last two. If the user has their browser in the "normal" view setting, the number of ads shown in the AdWords column is reduced to only four without scrolling! It gets even worse for content sites such as Internet news sites that may display only four advertisements per page! Therefore it's imperative that you rank at least in the top six spots on Google (top two in the blue rectangle and top four in the AdWords column) and content sites so that searchers are guaranteed to see your ad. If not, searchers may have to scroll down, which reduces the likelihood that your ad will be noticed. This is key to increasing your Quality Score.

## D. Amazing Flexibility of Google

The beauty of AdWords is that your advertising campaign can be changed at any time for free. Try to do that with traditional advertising, which is, for the most part, an unstoppable and unchangeable advertising juggernaut. Your marketing ad on a radio station will run for a set period such as 30 days. On Google you can change your ad every day or every hour if you are not getting the results you desire. You can also pause your ad at any time. Imagine being able to do this with a billboard that potentially reaches 2000 people and businesses every second.

### E. Smart Pricing Works 24/7/365

Google wants your advertising campaign to succeed. It uses a kind of digital natural selection process to keep the most popular ads on top. If your maximum Cost-Per-Click is too high, Google will automatically reduce it. That's right, Google will automatically *decrease* the amount you are paying for each click to the next highest bid. You'll be hard pressed to find a traditional marketing outlet that will do that for you.

Here's an example of Google's digital selection at work. Your maximum CPC is 31¢ to stay in the top spot and the second place ad drops the maximum amount it is willing to pay for each click from 30¢ to 25¢. Google will automatically drop your CPC to 26¢, but you will maintain the top spot on the search results page as long as you continue to get more clicks than your competitor.

Google's Smart Pricing automatically reduces your CPC to the lowest cost required for your ad to stay in its position on the search results page. In the marketing world this enables you to maximize your Return-on-Investment by targeting only customers interested in your designated keywords. Given the number of searches conducted on Google every day, the breadth of its partner sites, AdSense and the minimal costs, can your business afford not to use AdWords?

### YOUR ROI WILL CHANGE DAILY

Be mindful that if you advertise in foreign markets on Google your ROI will fluctuate daily based upon your home currency valuation. If you are located in Canada, but sell mostly to European customers, your ROI will change based on the strength of the Canadian dollar.

### F. How the Time of Day Affects Your CPC

Once advertisers' daily budgets are exhausted, their ads will stop running for the day. What this means for you is that you will be paying different amounts for clicks on your ad during the day. Let's say you have a competitor in your ad space with whom you are constantly battling for the top spot. When your competitor's daily budget is used up, your ad will automatically be bumped to the top spot and you will be paying less per click with Smart Pricing.

### BE MINDFUL OF THE BUDGET TOOL

An exception to the last example is when you or a competitor has the Budget Tool set for unlimited spending. In this case the ads will not stop during any part of the day.

### G. Google Sets the Frequency Your Ad Will Show

Google automatically spaces the times at which your ad will run if your daily budget is below the actual number of impressions your ad generates. For instance, if Google recommends a daily budget of $10 and you only select $5 a day, your ad will run half the time. Google tries to estimate the number of impressions for your ad based upon your daily budget and the estimated number of times your keywords will be searched in a given day. Don't be surprised if you run a search on your keyword one minute and your ad shows up, and then search again and no impression is shown.

Google tries to display ads evenly throughout the day so that your daily budget is not used up in the morning. This allows you to target customers who search at different hours. Say your maximum CPC is $.50 and you have a daily budget set at $12. If Google forecasts that you will receive twenty-four clicks a day, then when your ad initially begins, Google may display an impression once every hour. If the day is nearing its end and your ad has only received enough clicks to use up $6 of your $12, Google will begin showing more impressions. It's to Google's advantage and your advantage (if you have targeted the right market) to use up your daily budget in clicks. The way Google displays your ad is a steady, evenly paced marathon in the beginning of the day, and it becomes a race later in the day.

### SET DAILY BUDGET HIGH AT FIRST

> When you first begin your Google marketing campaign set your daily budget very high for a day or even a week to capture all the potential clicks you could be receiving. Once you determine that amount, you can optimize your daily budget accordingly.

It is important to realize that "Google time" is based off Pacific Standard Time (PST) in the United States. When the Google advertising day starts midnight PST, it is already 8 a.m. in parts of Europe. If you are targeting Europe and the U.S., your clicks could come very early in the day via Europe and you may have few left for advertising in the U.S.

### H. Bid Traps - How to Exploit & Prevent Them

In AdWords, Ad Rank is equal to the Quality Score (of which Click-Through-Rate is a component) times the minimum Cost-Per-Click.

$$\text{Ad Rank} = (\text{QS})(\text{Max. CPC})$$

Two advertisers with equal Quality Scores will merely compete on CPC. Remember that with Smart Pricing an advertiser paying a maximum of $3 per click (second advertiser paying $2 per click), will have their CPC rounded down to $0.01 over the second advertiser's CPC, which in this example would be $2.01. This has a domino effect for all advertisers down the line who are bidding on a particular keyword. Therefore, bid ceilings or traps are automatically created that you can use to your competitive advantage. Google certainly isn't going to tell you about this on their Website, but here is how to exploit them. Let's consider the keywords "Yahoo Domains" that triggers the following AdWord ads.

*Yahoo Domains $4.98* – Learn How to Get the Best Yahoo Domains.
www.[Website].com (Advertiser's Max Bid: $.90)

Yahoo Web Domains – Buy Yahoo Domains for Your Business Today.
www.[Website].com (Advertiser's Max Bid: $.32)

Yahoo Domains – Optimize Yahoo Domains Using this ebook Guide.
www.[Website].com (Advertiser's Max Bid: $.12)

Under this example the second bid will drop to $.13 per click since it will be discounted to be $.01 greater than the maximum bid of the next highest bidder to remain in its position. The top bid, although it's max bid is greatly higher at $.90, will drop to $.33 and will remain in the top position. The second bidder can take pride in only paying $.13 per click while the top bidder must pay over 100% more at $.33. The second bidder, realizing the great disparity between the second bidder's max bid and the first bidder's max bid, can further create a bid trap to make the top bidder pay even more per click. Here's how: If the second bidder raised its max bid to $.89, then the top bidder would be locked in to paying its max bid of $.90 for each click while the second bidder would still only pay $.13, which is $.01

greater than the max bid of the next highest bidder! Consider:

_Yahoo Domains $4.98_ – Learn How to Get the Best Yahoo Domains.
www.[Website].com (Advertiser's Max Bid: $.90)

Yahoo Web Domains – Buy Yahoo Domains for Your Business Today.
www.[Website].com (Advertiser's Max Bid: $.89)

Yahoo Domains – Optimize Yahoo Domains Using this ebook Guide.
www.[Website].com (Advertiser's Max Bid: $.12)

Bid traps are a great way to pop ballooning CPCs on AdWords.

## BID TRAPS DECREASE ROI

> Bid traps are a great way to decrease your competition's Return on Investment.

If you suspect a competitor has locked you into a bid trap, there is an easy way out. All you must do is reduce your maximum bid amount to $.01 below your competitor's. This will lock your competitor into paying higher click amounts and you will take advantage of the spread between your bid and the next maximum bid. Be mindful that if you are in the top spot, reducing your bid below the second spot will vault your competition into the top spot instead!

## BE CAREFUL OF BIDDING WARS

> Once bid traps are set and broken, bidding wars often begin that will eliminate any bid gaps among two competitors and the third maximum bid.

## III.  Ad Stylization Techniques

### A. Ad Title/Body/URL Lines Overview

Below is a representative AdWords promotion as it would appear in the right-hand column next to the Google search results. Following it is a demonstration on dos and don'ts for each line as well as optimization techniques.

| | | | |
|---|---|---|---|
| **Title Line:** | Entire Tales & Poems of Poe |  | Grab Attention |
| **Bodyline1:** | Photographic & Annotated | | Make Bodylines Flow |
| **Bodyline2:** | Edition. Be Afraid. Be Very Afraid! | | In Sentence Form |
| **URL Line:** | AndrewBarger.com | | Easy to Remember? |
| **Region Line:** | New York | | Location Region |

### 1. Title Line

The Title of your ad must grab attention immediately and distill your advertising message. There is no time to waste given the many ads that will be competing for precious user clicks. Google allows 25 characters on the Title Line, including spaces, so make each count. This is the only section of your ad that users click on to get to your Website so make it memorable.

### PLACE KEYWORDS IN YOUR TITLE

> The highest performing ads have keywords in the Title, which means they are bolded when impressions are shown. This is one of the most important factors in getting your ad clicked on.

Let's consider a Title for the keyword "eloan" for the e-loan credit industry. Note how the keyword is bolded by Google, which makes the ad standout in the AdWords column.

Good Title: **Eloan** Store

Better Title: Need **Eloan**? **Eloan** Store

We have used the keyword twice in the Title, which creates two bolded words in the Title alone! Customers view ads with bolded keywords as being of high quality.

### CAPITALIZE WORDS IN YOUR TITLE

> Capitalize Title Line words to make your ad stand apart.

Even Better Title: <u>Got **Eloans**? **Eloan** Store</u>

### MAKE THE KEYWORD FIRST IN YOUR TITLE

> Some of the highest CTRs result from having the keyword first in the Title Line. Since users read from left to right, make the keyword the first word in your Title.

Superior Title: <u>**Eloan** Store-Got **Eloans?**</u>

### 2. Bodylines

The two AdWord lines that form the body of the text are the substance of your advertisement. Here is where you define why your product or services is the best. You have 70 total characters in which to accomplish this (35 per line) so your message must be fine-tuned. In addition, the Bodylines should flow and have proper sentence structure. Remember that if you have one of the top two AdWords positions, your ads will show in the coveted blue rectangle at the top of Google's search results.

### ALL KEYWORDS BOLDED

Keywords anywhere in the ad will be bolded regardless of order. If the keywords are "Domain Name Registrar," Bodylines with the text "**Name** is King in **Domain** Game. Visit This **Registrar**." Will have the keywords bolded. This means that the order of the keywords you bid on does not matter as every one is bolded no matter what order they appear in the ad.

It's not recommended to make the Title Line and Bodylines one long sentence because of the way AdWords impressions are shown within the Google Search Network. For instance, AOL places the Title Line and Bodylines on one line, separated by a semicolon. If you make your Title and Bodylines one long sentence, you will have a semicolon appearing in the middle of them on AOL. Google itself separates the Title and Bodylines for ads in the blue rectangle, but the Body does not start beneath the Title. Instead, the URL is the text under the Title. Making the Title and Bodylines one long sentence will make your ad choppy and ultimately decrease the perception of your product or service quality. Make the Bodylines one long sentence or separate the Bodylines with punctuation. Many companies in the Search Network put the Title and URL lines on the same line, separated by a hyphen, Bodylines underneath. This enables search engines to maximize the number of Google advertisements that fit on a searcher's screen.

## ORDER OF THE BODYLINES IS IMPORTANT

Increase your CTR by merely switching the order in which your Bodylines are placed within the ad. Get your key marketing phrase *beneath* the Title Line if there is no keyword in the Title. Remember, Internet users scan even quicker than someone looking at a newspaper so getting your attention grabbing ideas pushed to the top left of the ad will increase your clicks. This miniature ad heat map is the same used for Google's Search Results page. Users begin reading from the top left.

Spread out keywords to draw attention. If the keyword appears in the Title and *both* Bodylines, form a > type arrangement of keywords within the ad. This is best seen in the examples below:

<u>**Eloan** Store</u>
Inexpensive **Eloan**.
Low Closing. Signup Now.
[Website].com

Here the highlighted keywords take on a backslash (\) look through the ad to gain attention on each side of the ad. This is good keyword balancing.

<u>**Eloan** Store</u>
Inexpensive **Eloan**.
**Eloan**-Signup Online!
[Website].com

With the keyword bolded on each line and Eloan in the first Bodyline offset to the right, the forward arrow (**>**) formation enhances the keyword focus of the ad instead of the keywords being stacked one on top of the other.

<u>**Eloan** Store-Got **Eloan**?</u>
30% Off **Eloan**.
**Eloan** Quick at **Eloan** Store.
[Website].com

This may seem like keyword overkill, but if you can get your marketing message across and still use numerous keyword placements within the ad, all the better. Notice the (X) spacing of the keywords.

### 3. URL Line

Similar to the Bodylines, the URL line is limited to 35 characters. It must include the domain extension, for example: .com, .net, .org, or .biz. The linking address, which may be different than your URL Line, must link to an active Website. You must pause any ad linking to a site that is under construction or down for maintenance. In addition, you cannot link to an email address or a file (e.g., an image, audio, video, or document file that requires an additional program or application to open or run it).

## DISPLAY DOMAIN NAMES WITH RELEVANCE

> If offering computer consulting services, a high-tech sounding domain name will get more clicks on an identical ad than a low-tech name.

It's interesting to note that Google does not allow you to click on the URL line, only the Title. The key for this line is to get people to remember your URL even after they have logged off the Internet and also to have a domain name that indicates your specialty in the products or services you're offering. Even if a keyword is part of your URL, that part of the URL will not be bolded by Google.

## KEEP YOUR LISTED DOMAIN NAME AS SHORT AS POSSIBLE

> If people can simply type in BottleTreeBooks.com to visit your Website, do not put www.BottleTreeBooks.com on the URL line, or worse yet http://www.BottleTreeBooks.com The hypertext protocol and World Wide Web letters only serve as a barrier to people remembering your Website address!

Google does not allow pop-up ads on the linking page. How does Google define "pop-ups"? Any window, regardless of content, that is opened in addition to the regular window upon entering or leaving the linked page. The back button must also be enabled at your linking Website so that users can easily return to the Google search page or ad network page. Finally, your site should use a secure server (https://) when collecting personal information from Google users.

### 4. Region Line

As will be discussed in greater detail below, Google allows you to specify the region in which your ad will run when searched on by people in that region. If you run a Google Local ad, Google will display the city or metropolitan region on the last line of the ad. You will have no control over this line, but its inclusion by Google makes your ad stand apart from the others because it has five lines instead of the four traditional lines.

### B. Definitive Ad Stylization

The way in which AdWord ads are stylized is key to making your ad stand apart. If you pick wrongly, your ad will seem like a blur of words and characters that will blend in with all the other ads. If you select your words and stylization correctly, your ad will convey more of your marketing message and stand apart from the rest of the ads. Highly optimized ads will get you the most clicks even if you do not have top placement within the AdWords column.

### USE GRAMMAR & SPELL CHECK

Cut and paste spell-checked and grammar-checked verbiage into a new ad. For the majority of Internet customers your ads will be their first introduction to your products and services. A spelling mistake in a small Internet ad is the equivalent of having a large, misspelled business sign outside your office.

## 1. Style/Interior Punctuation

**Fonts**: The AdWords default font is Times New Roman, regular, 10 point. This cannot be changed.

**Capitals**: Capitals can be used in AdWords. The first letter of *each* word is permitted to be a capital and is a great way to make your ad stand out from all the others.

**Stylization**: Bold/Italics/Underlines/Small Caps/Bullets cannot be copied into AdWords from a word processing program such as Microsoft Word.

**Commas**: Avoid the serial comma. It uses a precious character.

| Good | Bad |
|---|---|
| Benchmark Lending<br>Loans, CDs and Refinancing.<br>Signup Online-Fast.<br>[Website].com | Benchmark Lending and CDs<br>Loans, CDs, and refinancing.<br>Signup online–fast.<br>http:\\www.[Website].com |
| **Why?** | **Why?** |
| • Capitalization of each word.<br>• No use of serial comma (1 char. saved).<br>• Essential part of domain name used (11 char. saved). | • No capitalization of each word.<br>• Use of the serial comma.<br>• URL Line has unnecessary characters (http: \\www.). |

## 2. Style/Interior Punctuation Continued

**Apostrophes**:     Avoid use with decades or acronyms.

**Semicolons**:     Semicolons may be used. Note that a semicolon uses two characters versus a hyphen not surrounded by spaces.

**Hyphens**:     Do not use spaces surrounding your hyphen. It wastes two precious characters you might need later.

**Slashes**:     Slashes are not allowed outside of the URL Line.

**Spaces**:     Spaces must be used in normal context on the Title Line. Use only one space after a period instead of two.

| Good | Bad |
|---|---|
| Benchmark Lending<br>Loans, CDs & Refinancing.<br>Signup Online-Fast. 90s Rates.<br>[Website].com | Loans - Benchmark Lending<br>Loans/CDs.<br>Signup online – fast. 90's Rates.<br>[Website].com |
| **Why?** | **Why?** |
| • No spaces around hyphen (2 char. saved).<br>• No slash.<br>• No apostrophe in decade. | • Improper use of spaces in title.<br>• Slash used improperly.<br>• Spaces surrounding the hyphen.<br>• Apostrophe used in decade. |

## 3. Abbreviations/Shorthand/Symbols

Shorthand and symbols (found under the Insert dropdown in Word and WordPerfect) can be used in the proper context.

**+:**                  Use as addition symbol, or instead of "plus."

**Lb:**                 Exchange for weight "pound."

**£:**                  Exchange for monetary "pound."

**Nos or #:**           Truncate "numbers."

**Large Numbers:**      Use "100s" instead of "hundreds;" "1000s" instead of "thousands."

**TV:**                 Instead of "television."

**CD:**                 Instead of "Compact Disc" or "CD-ROM."

**Countries/States:**   Use country abbreviations like UK instead of "United Kingdom." Use state abbreviations such as TN instead of Tennessee.

**$:**                  Only use to denote dollars (e.g., $10.99), do not use to replace "money" or "price."

## PLACE SYMBOLS IN YOUR TEXT AD TO GET ATTENTION

> The trick to getting symbols in your ad is to copy and paste them from a word processing document. Some of Google's syndication partners may not display them, however, so keep this in mind.

| Good | Bad |
|---|---|
| Workout Depot #1 Brands<br>+ Size Clothes-All Dumbbell Lbs.<br>Low Prices. As Seen on TV.<br>[Website].com | Workout Depot–Best Brands<br>Plus size clothing. As seen on TV.<br>All Dumbbell Pounds. Low $.<br>http:\\www.[Website].com |
| **Why?** | **Why?** |
| • # used for "number" (5 char. saved).<br>• + instead of "Plus" (3 char. saved).<br>• Lbs replaced "pounds" (3 char. saved).<br>• Prices spelled out.<br>• TV used for "television" (10 char. saved). | • Best used instead of the shorter "#1," which also draws more attention.<br>• Spelled out "pounds."<br>• $ is improper in this context.<br>• Television spelled out. |

## 4. Abbreviations/Shorthand/Symbols Continued

| | |
|---|---|
| **%:** | Insert for "percentage." |
| ***@*:** | Replaces "at." |
| **?:** | Use instead of "question." |
| **&:** | Never waste characters by spelling out "and." Use the ampersand instead. |
| **0-10:** | Use instead of spelling out the number. |

Special typographical fonts will not be displayed in AdWords. Fonts such as Webdings and Wingdings cannot be displayed in your Google ad. Cutting and pasting these symbols will result in the underlying character being placed in the ad instead of the symbol.

| Good | Bad |
|---|---|
| Benchmark Lending & CDs<br>8 Loan Types: 20% Off.<br>High Quality @ Low Prices.<br>[Website].com | Benchmark Lending and CDs<br>Eight Loans-Twenty Percent Off.<br>High Quality at Low Prices.<br>[Website].com |
| **Why?** | **Why?** |
| • & exchanged for "and" (2 char. saved).<br>• 8 substituted for "eight" (4 char. saved).<br>• 20 replaced "Twenty" (4 char. saved).<br>• % used for "Percent" (7 char. saved).<br>• @ used for "at" (1 char. saved). | • Used "and."<br>• Spelled out "Eight."<br>• Used "Twenty."<br>• Spelled out "Percent."<br>• At used instead of "@." |

## PLACE LOCAL REGION NAME IN TEXT AD

If you offer a local service or product, include the name in the ad. Potential local customers in Memphis are much more likely to click on an ad with "Memphis" than a generic, national sounding ad.

| Good | Bad |
|---|---|
| Benchmark Lending for Less<br>Memphis BBQ Kit w/Loan!<br>Never a ? of Trust.<br>[Website].com | Benchmark Lending 4 Less<br>Free BBQ Kit with Loan!<br>See Our Gr8 Prices!<br>[Website].com |
| **Why?** | **Why?** |
| • Memphis region defined.<br>• CD substituted for "compact disk" (10 char. saved).<br>• W/ replaces "with" (2 char. saved).<br>• ? used instead of "Question" (7 char. saved). | • No mention of local region.<br>• 4 not used in number context and is not allowed.<br>• Excessive use of shorthand makes ad unprofessional.<br>• "gr8" is not used in normal context. "License plate" lingo is not allowed. |

## 5. Legal Terminology

**Registered Trademarks**: ® - registered trademark or service mark.

**Non-Registered Marks**: tm – unregistered trademark and (sm) denotes an unregistered service mark.

**Copyrights**: © replaces copyright.

### SEARCH TRADEMARKS FOR FREE

You can search registered trademarks for free at the U.S. Patent & Trademark Office: www.USPTO.gov. Canada http://strategis.ic.gc.ca/ also offers trademark searches. Here is Australia's official Website www.IPAustralia.gov.au for searching. In Europe, you can search Community Trademarks for free at the European Union http://oami.eu.int/en/default.htm. In Asia, you can search trademarks in China at www.ChinaTrademarkOffice.com. India also has a searchable trademark database: www.Skorydov.com/tmr.

Read Google's policy for using trademarks in your ad or keywords: http://www.google.com/tm_complaint_adwords.html At present,

Google will investigate complaints from trademark owners only related to trademarks used within AdWords text and it will suspend the ad in its discretion. If suspended, an advertiser must submit a new ad with the trademark term deleted. Google is trying to prevent confusion in the marketplace, a hallmark of trademark infringement. For instance, if the trademark Coke is used in an ad, but the company only sells Pepsi products, then searchers may be confused in clicking on the ad in the mistaken belief they will find Coke products for sale.

Google does not limit the use of trademarks as underlying keywords. This does not mean, however, that competitors will agree with their trademarked keywords being used to drive traffic to a competitive site, so use caution.

### NO USE OF "GOOGLE" IN ADWORDS

Use of "Google" in an AdWords ad will automatically get the ad rejected by Google's editors. Google keeps tight wraps on the use of its corporate identity. Interestingly, other Google trademarks such as "AdWords" and "AdSense" may be used in ads.

Note that Google's Trademark Complaint Procedure www.google.com/tm_complaint.html varies for trademark rights in the U.S. and Canada, versus trademark rights elsewhere.

### SEARCH YELLOW PAGES & WHITE PAGES AROUND THE WORLD

There may be instances when you need to check if a business exists in a local market before starting your Google marketing campaign. www.Argali.com offers free yellow and white page searches from over 20 online information sources.

| Good | Bad |
|---|---|
| "Coffee w/Poe"-Amazon.com® <br> Historical Novel of Poe's Life, <br> Loves & Letters! © Andrew Barger. <br> [Website].com | "Coffee w/Poe"-Amazon.com <br> Historical Novel of Poe's Life. <br> Copyright-Andrew Barger. <br> [Website].com |
| **Why?** | **Why?** |
| • ® denotes registered trademark. <br> • Bodylines flow together. <br> • © replaces Copyright (8 char. saved). | • No trademark designations noted. <br> • Copyright is spelled out. |

## 6. Punctuation & Contractions

**Periods:** Use at the end of Bodylines to make them read as sentences. Alternatively, one long sentence can span the first and second Bodylines. Use only one space after a period in your ad instead of the traditional two spaces.

**Exclamations:** The Title cannot have an exclamation point and the Bodylines may only have one exclamation point.

**Question Marks:** No limits as long as used appropriately.

**Repetition:** Doubling of punctuation/words is not allowed.

**Contractions:** Use these negative-sounding words sparingly.

| Good | Bad |
|---|---|
| Benchmark Lending & CDs<br>20 Loans: 20% Off!<br>Why Go Anywhere Else?<br>[Website].com | Benchmark Lending & CDs!<br>20 Loans-20% Off<br>Low, Low, Low $-Intrigued??<br>[Website].com |
| **Why?** | **Why?** |
| <ul><li>No exclamation in Title Line.</li><li>Exclamation used at end of 1st Bodyline.</li><li>No unnecessary repetition.</li><li>Single Question mark is proper.</li></ul> | <ul><li>Exclamation point not allowed in Title Line.</li><li>No use of period at end of 1st Bodyline so it will not read like a sentence when combined with the 2nd Bodyline.</li><li>Invalid repetition of "Low."</li><li>Double question marks are not allowed.</li></ul> |

## USE TELEPHONE NUMBERS IN YOUR AD

Use of numbers in your ad is a great way to save precious characters *and* to make it stand apart. If your business has an 800 number, use it in your AdWords campaign! The string of numbers will make your ad stand out and provide another means for customers to contact you who may have security concerns about giving information via the Internet. If advertising on Google Local, a regional telephone number is the best way for customers to reach you and the local area code will identify you with that region.

If only minor changes are required (e.g., removing a question mark or correcting a spelling mistake) for an ad to comply with Google's Editorial Guidelines, an AdWords Specialist may edit your ad. Google will not, however, take responsibility for fixing all ads. Ensure your advertisement meets the Editorial Guidelines prior to running the ad so that it does not get suspended while your competitors are getting clicks.

## 7. Call-to-Action & Generic Words

**"Click Now"**:       Improper Call-to-Action.
**"Click Here"**:       Improper Call-to-Action.
**"Click on Me"**:       Improper Call-to-Action.
**"Look Here"**:       Improper Call-to-Action.
**"Visit Here"**:       Improper Call-to-Action.
**"Look at This"**:       Improper Call-to-Action.
**"L@@K"**:       Improper Call-to-Action.
**"This Site is"**:       Improper generic phrase; could apply to any ad.
**The second Bodyline cannot extend into the URL line.**

| Good | Bad |
|---|---|
| Benchmark Loans<br>20 Loans: 20% Off!<br>Visit the Home Loan Specialist.<br>[Website].com | Benchmark Loans!<br>20 Loans-20% Off<br>Look at Me to See what you<br>Need. [Website].com |
| **Why?** | **Why?** |
| • Proper call to action based on unique business model. | • Improper call-to-action.<br>• Bodyline 2 bleeds into the URL line. |

No inappropriate language is allowed in AdWords, including swearing or language that is deemed offensive (i.e., politically incorrect). Be careful of what region your ads are targeted as some words may be offensive there. "Bloody" is a curse word in the UK but not in the US.

---

**Three Categories of Ads**

Ads are placed into three special categories by Google's editors:

1. Family Safe
2. Non-Family Safe
3. Adult Sexual Content

Google allows all three types of ads, but its partners on the Google Network may not.

---

If you want to make claims in AdWords that your product or service is better than your competitor's, you must have factual data on the Web page customers will first see when clicking on your ad. This could take the form of test data or a performance chart. Avoid puffery. Comparative or subjective phrases such as "Best," "Cheapest," "Top," or "#1," must be verified on your Website by a third party.

## IV.  Keyword Creation and Management

### A. Keywords Are Key

Google rewards relevance and relevance comes by fine-tuning your ads to appear when keywords (i.e., search terms) are used linking your products or services to potential customer interests. Not only are keywords of primary importance, but also the type of ad. You can choose the most relevant keywords in the world, but if your ad is not compelling, potential customers will not click on it.

There are two ways you can approach your initial marketing campaign on Google: Use a few, highly targeted keywords or use a large number of keywords, selecting both specific and broad keywords so that you can later funnel your keywords to the ones resulting in the best ROI. The approach you select depends on your target market. We'll discuss each in detail below.

### 1. Highly Targeted Keywords Campaign

When a Google advertising campaign is first started it is normal to choose broad or generic search terms so that an advertisement is displayed numerous times. This catchall tactic is absolutely the wrong one to take if you are marketing specific products. If you have a defined market and specific products or services for that market, start your campaign with a few highly targeted keywords. If you are offering Washington D.C. laser hair removal, target the keywords "Washington D.C. laser hair removal," "Washington DC laser hair removal," "Washington DC lazer hair removal," and "Washington DC hair removal," "DC laser hair removal," etc. There is no need to apply a dragnet approach to advertising this very specific product that is targeted at an equally specific market.

If, for example, you were marketing soccer gear, the generic keyword "soccer" would be too broad. Under this scenario your ads would appear when people searched on the terms "soccer moms" "soccer stadiums," "rules of soccer," etc. Your ads would appear for terms not associated with your business and that are unlikely to increase business. The ads would rank low in the AdWords column because they would have a low CTR. And, even if users did click on your ad, they would be unlikely to buy your products, which means you would be wasting ad dollars in the form of low ROI.

## DESIGNATE A SEPARATE CPC FOR EACH KEYWORD

Google's Power Posting Tool allows you to set a unique CPC for *each* keyword. If you have a highly targeted ad campaign, designate a separate CPC for each keyword. If your average position is shown to be low on the Traffic Estimator Tool, increase the amount per click you are willing to pay for that keyword. If you already have the #1 position when only paying $.05 per click, there is no reason to pay Google more. You would be throwing money away. In addition, be aware that Google always rounds up your bid amount to the nearest hundredth place. For instance, a $.075 USD per click bid will be rounded up to $.08 USD.

When editing your keywords, you can designate different hyperlinks for different keywords even though the identical ad impression will be shown. For example, if your Website specializes in offering all types of gift cards, most generic gift card ads would link to your home page. If, however, a person types in the keywords "Best Buy gift card" you can link it to your Best Buy gift card page within your Website. Google makes a seemingly difficult task easy.

When you set up your AdWords campaign the Keyword Tool will display the average number of searches users conduct on that term every day, suggest related keywords, and allow you to get an estimated average CPC and ad position based your maximum CPC.

There is no need for a shotgun approach to advertising with Google. Your exact target market is defined! Here is a sample keyword variation on the medical term mesothelioma.

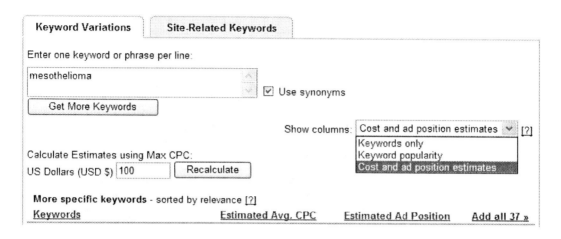

The Keyword Tool revealed thirty-seven variations on that keyword. This is a very powerful tool in your AdWords arsenal that is available for free. Let's say you are a mesothelioma attorney or doctor bidding on the keyword mesothelioma. Instead of using the broad keyword "mesothelioma" use the following specific keywords:

- Peritoneal Mesothelioma
- Pleural Mesothelioma
- Malignant Pleural Mesothelioma
- Mesothelioma Research

You can then further narrow the times when your ad is triggered for these keywords by using Exact Match or Phrase Match, which is discussed below. In this example mesothelioma attorneys or doctors specializing in mesothelioma treatment can better focus their keywords to get clicks in their specialty and weed out clicks by, for example, medical students who do not have the disease and are in no need of mesothelioma attorneys or doctors specializing in mesothelioma treatment.

If you can find keywords that your competitors have missed, or that have few others bidding on them, you will have much less competition when impressions of your ad are shown on Google.

## RUN KEYWORDS IN OTHER COUNTRIES

A great way to find alternate keywords is to plug your broad keywords into the Keyword Tool and designate a search for a foreign country. For example, if you are advertising for the UK market, plugging in your keywords for the US market may yield other search terms competitors are not using in the UK.

## 2. Traffic Estimator Assistance

Okay, this begs the question as to how you can learn which keywords your competitors are bidding on? It's simple. Use Google's Traffic Estimator Tool that is located under the Tools bar within the Campaign Management tab.

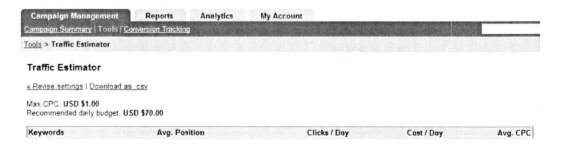

You will also be presented with the Traffic Estimator Tool when setting up a new Ad Group. It is now pseudo-integrated into the new ad set up process. We will discuss the Traffic Estimator Tool in greater detail later in this book.

Here's an example of what the Traffic Estimator Tool may return for Google Affiliates:

| | Clicks / Day | Avg. CPC | Cost / Day | Avg. Position |
|---|---|---|---|---|
| London Google Affiliates | < 0.1 | $0.05 | $0.00 | 30.3 |
| Google Affiliates | 7.1 | $0.05 | $0.36 | 6.9 |
| UK Google Affiliates | < 0.1 | $0.05 | $0.00 | 1.0 |
| Google Affiliate | < 0.1 | $0.05 | $0.00 | 2.4 |

This simple chart tells us volumes about a potential marketing campaign for Google affiliates.

### a. Clicks/Day

Under this column the keywords "Google Affiliates" will garner over 7 forecasted clicks per day while the others will result in less than .1 clicks. Right away we see that this is where the most searches are conducted. But if you specialize in a UK based Google affiliate program, this may result in clicks and ad money spent on people in foreign countries searching for Google affiliate programs.

### b. Avg. CPC

Here is the average Cost-Per-Click Google estimates for these keywords.

### c. Cost/Day

We see that the keywords "Google Affiliates" will gain the most clicks and result in $0.36 being spent per day.

### d. Avg. Position

This column ranks the average position in which your ad impression will be placed in the AdWords column. Note that the keywords resulting in the most clicks will not necessarily result in the lowest placement. "London Google Affiliates" has less than .01 forecasted clicks per day yet the average position is a low 30.3 at $.05 per click. What does this tell us? Competitors are paying large sums per click for the keywords "London Google Affiliates" when the most traffic is under "Google Affiliates." Look for similar opportunities in your market area.

## REMEMBER YOUR COMPANY AND BRAND NAMES

When sifting through hundreds of potential keywords it is easy to forget those right under your nose. Do not forget to bid on your company name and brand names as keywords to ensure people looking for your products can find you instead of your competitors.

## 3. Keyword Funneling Campaign

If your products or services cater to a large number of potential customers, pick at least 50 keywords and then cull them down to the top 10 or 15 that are getting you the most ROI. The mistake many advertisers make is trying to pin down the top 10 keywords from the *start*, which is difficult at best until a click-through track record has been established. For instance, if you sell many types of hammers, you may list the normal keywords such as "claw hammers," "sledge hammers," "ball ping hammers," etc. A better initial keyword campaign would include those keywords plus others such as "rubber hammers," "metal hammers," "discount hammers," "mallets," "hammer enthusiasts," "hammer collectors," "Stanley hammers," "Black & Decker hammers," etc. You may learn that the Internet is full of users searching under "mallets" instead of "rubber hammers."

The downside to broad keywords, as will be discussed in greater detail below, is that they may lead to mis-clicks. For instance, if your business is antiquities and you're offering President Abraham Lincoln memorabilia, the broad keyword "Lincoln" may attract mis-clicks by those interested in Lincoln automobiles or Lincoln, Nebraska. Avoid unwanted clicks by people who are unlikely to buy your product or services. The ultimate goal with Google advertising is not to increase visits to your Website but rather to increase sales.

### 4. Similar Keywords

In addition to focusing your broad search term on more specific terms, Google also provides a selection of similar keywords within the results of its Keyword Tool. These will not contain your broad search term, but will offer search terms that are close. Note that most of the similar terms will be relevant, but some are clearly not within a particular industry and you can cull these immediately. Conducting a broad search on "hammers" under Google's Keyword Tool resulted in the suggestion of four "more specific keywords" and over a hundred "similar keywords."

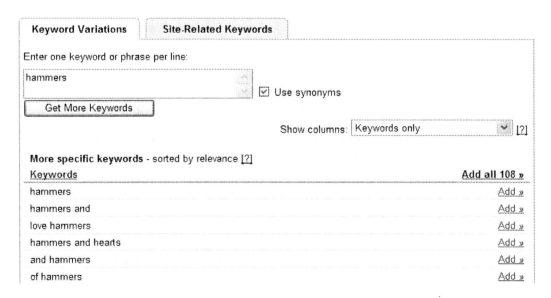

## 5. Keyword Matching Options

Change keyword matching options to better target your ads. By specifying the types of keyword matching options that will trigger your ads, you can widen or narrow your focus to prospective customers.

| Four Keyword Matching Options | |
| --- | --- |
| a. Broad/Expanded | Input: **Keyword** |
| b. Phrase | Input: **"Keyword"** |
| c. Exact | Input: **[Keyword]** |
| d. Negative | Input: **-Keyword** |

### NO KEYWORD MATCHING ON THE CONTENT NETWORK

Keyword matching does not apply to AdWord ads on Google's Content Network.

Use the Traffic Estimator Tool to get an initial idea of how much traffic will come your way by using the various keyword matching options.

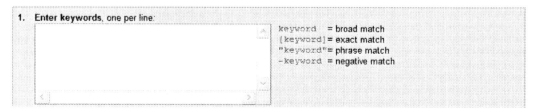

**Traffic Estimator**

Get quick traffic estimates for new keywords without adding them to an account or using the AdWords sign-up wizard.

1. Enter keywords, one per line:

keyword = broad match
[keyword] = exact match
"keyword"= phrase match
-keyword = negative match

## a. Broad Match

Broad Match is the biggest net you have as an advertiser to gain customers. On the Search Network, however, it is too big and not recommended. With the Broad Match net you will likely catch Internet users that are not interested in your products or services, which is simply a waste of your advertising money. On the Search Network, you want to catch the big fish (i.e., those likely to buy your products or services) and let the little ones (i.e., those out for a leisurely Internet stroll and who are unlikely to buy your products or services) swim through your net. Here's an example: Say you are a surgeon who specializes in various eye surgeries such as cataract surgery, and lasik surgery. Your Broad Match keywords are "Eye Surgery." This means that impressions of your ad will show for the keyword "Eye" or "Surgery" even if other words are included in the search. Under this example impressions of the ad would show for "Eyeglasses," "Plastic Surgery," and "Sinus Surgery." Needless to say, your ad would have a low CTR on the Search Network for these Broad Match terms and your Quality Score would plummet. A few people, however, searching for eyeglasses may actually decide to click on your ad and get lasik surgery.

## NO KEYWORD MATCHING ON THE CONTENT NETWORK

> Your keyword is your keyword on the Content Network. There is no keyword matching.

## b. Expanded Match

If you select Broad Matching, your keywords will *automatically* be included in Expanded Matching. This means Google's computer algorithms will show impressions of your ad for keywords that closely match your selected keywords or that are slight variations. Consider the keywords "Lasik Surgery." Expanded Matching includes synonyms (Lasik, Lazik, Lasick, Lazick) related phrases (Lasik Eye Surgery, Lasik Surgery in New York, New York Lasik Centers), and plurals (Lasik Surgeries). Expanded matching allows your ad to show more often and be linked to search terms that are relevant to your marketing campaign. Under Expanded Match the keywords "Eye Surgery" may result in impressions of your ad showing when "Lasik Surgery" is searched on.

### HOW TO STOP EXPANDED MATCHING

Adding them as negative keywords can stop Expanded Match terms. You can also change Broad Match keywords to Exact or Phrase Match keywords to eliminate Expanded Matching.

Google will automatically change Expanded Matches over time based upon which keywords best fit the intent of your ad. This artificial intelligence feature shows your ad for only the alternate keywords and phrases that are getting you the most clicks. It also learns additional keywords and phrases to show your ad when searched upon. Remember, the more clicks your ad gets, the more money Google makes. Google wants your ad to succeed!

### c. Phrase Match

Phrase Match requires that the *exact keywords*, in the *exact order* must be included in the search for an impression of your ad to show. Other words may also be included. For instance, let's consider our "Lasik Surgery" example. Under this scenario the search term "Lasik Surgery Centers" would trigger an impression of your ad, but "Lasik Centers for Surgery" would not.

### NO EXPANDED MATCHING FOR PHRASE MATCH

Expanded Matching is not available for Phrase Match.

### d. Exact Match

Exact Match means just what it says. The *exact keywords* must be used in the search and the keywords must be in the *exact order, without any other words*. If the Exact Match Keywords are "Lasik Surgery," then "California Lasik Surgery" will not invoke an impression of your ad and neither will "Lasik Surgeries."

Consider the following chart using "Lasik Surgery" as an example for keywords. The chart shows when an impression of the ad would be shown on the following search terms.

| Search Term | Broad Match | Expanded Match | Phrase Match | Exact Match |
|---|---|---|---|---|
| Lasik Surgeries | Yes | Yes | No | No |
| California Lasik | Yes | Yes | No | No |
| New York Lasik Surgery | Yes | Yes | Yes | No |
| Lasik Surgery | Yes | Yes | Yes | Yes |

### e. Negative Match

Negative keywords are a great way to prevent wasted clicks that drain your advertising budget. You can use Negative Match in addition to one of the other keyword matching options. We've discussed how to disable Expanded Match with Negative Match. There are certain instances where you want to use Negative Match to ensure ads do not appear when your company is discussed online

#### USE NEGATIVE KEYWORDS TO DISASSOCIATE TERMS

If there has been negative media press relating to your industry as a whole, you may not want your ads showing for certain negative keywords such as "investigation" or "disappointing earnings" etc.

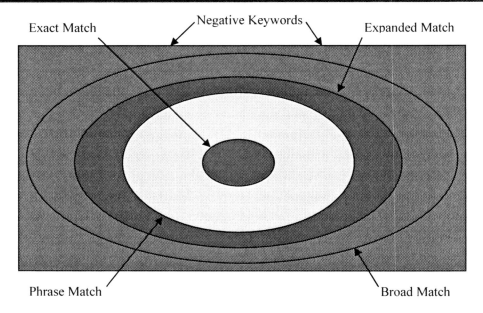

Remember that Negative Match will ultimately reduce the number of impressions of your ad and therefore the number of clicks. We are seeking *quality* clicks that are likely to result in sales. With negative keywords, watch your clicks and advertising dollars decrease, but sales increase! You get the best of all worlds.

## USE THE KEYWORD TOOL TO FIND NEGATIVE KEYWORDS

Plugging "Lasik Surgery" into Google's Keyword Tool will also list many similar terms. If these are not relevant to the specific type of shoes you are selling, ad them as *negative* keywords.

## B. Abbreviations, Plurals and Misspellings
Google's advertising system is centered on performance. The ads getting the clicks are the ones that receive top placement. That's why it is essential that your ad stick out from the others. Below are tips on how to make it happen. If you have a low Quality Score, your ad can stop running for certain keywords unless you keep paying more per click!

Abbreviations, plurals and misspellings are a great way to get additional clicks on certain keywords and phrases that your competitors may not cover. Google's Keyword Tool will suggest these variations for you! Use the Keyword Tool in combination with your own industry knowledge to select keywords that your competitors are missing.

## Use Abbreviations, Plurals and Misspellings

An eye surgeon might include the following keywords in their Ad Group for lasik:

> Lasik *(Correct Spelling)*
> Lasiks *(Plural)*
> Lasick *(Common Misspelling)*
> Inexpensive Lasik *(Additional Words)*
> Inexpensive Lazik *(Additional Words Included with Plurals or Misspellings)*

Remember that if you are using Broad Match, Expanded Match will include these variations for you.

### CREATE AN AD GROUP FOR EACH SET OF KEYWORDS

Instead of having one ad of which identical impressions are shown for *every* keyword, breakdown the keywords by specific groups and have tailored ads for each. If your business is retailing and you sell various items of coats, create specific ads for "winter coats," "parkas," "raincoats," "windbreakers," etc.

Below are examples of Ad Groups set up for "Lasik" eye surgery and variations of the keyword that a competitor may not consider, including a misspelling.

Keyword: **Lasik** – Search Term: **Lasik**

| Ad Group 1 |
| --- |
| **Lasik**-Low Cost<br>20-25% Off **Lasik**.<br>**Lasik**-California!<br>[Website].com |

- Title includes exact plural keyword, which means it will be bolded.
- Keyword used again in Bodylines. Note the (>) keyword configuration within the ad.

## ONE LETTER MAKES ALL THE DIFFERENCE

When a search is conducted, Google bolds words in your ad that exactly match words in the search. Lack of *one* letter can make your ad get lost in the AdWords shuffle. Google will not highlight "Equity Loans" on a search for "Equity Loan." Likewise, "Equity Loan" will not be bolded on a search for "Equity Loans." This AdWords shortcoming can be remedied if you slightly change your ad for various plurals that will allow key terms in your ad to be highlighted by Google.

---

Keyword: **Lasik** – Search Term: **Lazik**

---

**Ad Group 2**

**<u>Lazik</u>**
20-50% Off Lasik.
Get Lasik Now!
[Website].com

- Title matches misspelled keyword, which means it will be bolded.
- Keyword is spelled correctly in Bodylines, but they will not be bolded.

In two instances customers will misspell your keyword when searching. The first is the obvious typo situation where they hit the wrong key. The second is when they are unsure of how to spell the keyword/product name. This is the only time you want a typo reflected in your ad, but limit it only to the Title. If you set up an Ad Group for each primary misspelling of your product name and include it in only the Title, in the vast majority of instances your ad will be the *only* one with the term highlighted! Then use the correct spelling in the Bodylines just in case the potential customer is the first type of searcher and realizes they made a typo. This is a great way to advertise when your competitors may not think to do so and to make your ad stand apart with a bold misspelled keyword in the Title even if they do!

## REMEMBER NUMBER ABBREVIATIONS

If you are bidding on the keywords "Second Mortgage," remember numerical abbreviations. You should also bid on "2nd Mortgage." Internet users sometimes take the lazy path to search for products and services.

| Keyword: **Lasik** – Search Term: **Lasik Surgery** |
| --- |

| **Ad Group 4** |
| --- |
| **Lasik** Surgery<br>10-20% Off **Lasik** Surgery.<br>**Lasik** Surgery-New York!<br>[Website].com |
| &bull;   Title matches keywords, which means they will be bolded.<br>&bull;   Keywords used again in Bodylines, which means they will be bolded. |

Obviously more Ad Groups can be created for the Mallet example above following this same line of logic. See what works best for your marketing campaign based off these techniques.

### C. Holiday Ads

Holiday ads fuel many businesses. Some are season-only businesses, such as year around Christmas stores and fruitcake bakeries. They depend on the holidays for most of their sales. With this in mind, we are giving the holiday advertising season the attention it deserves.

### BEGIN SEASONAL ADS EARLY

Under a Shop.org poll, only 22% of sellers begin their holiday marketing by mid-October, yet over 50% of holiday shoppers have already begun to shop. Beat your competition to the holiday marketplace by starting your holiday ads in early October!

**Products Purchased Online, 2003 and 2005 – Leading Categories**

| Product Category | 2003 (%) | 2005 (%) | |
|---|---|---|---|
| Photo/Supplies | 21 | 35 | +14 |
| Office Supplies/ Stationery | 31 | 44 | +13 |
| Electronics | 41 | 52 | +11 |
| Home Furnishings | 26 | 36 | +10 |
| Prescriptions | 13 | 23 | +10 |
| Jewelry/Watches | 22 | 31 | +9 |
| Greeting Cards | 9 | 18 | +9 |
| Home Décor | 34 | 42 | +8 |
| Travel | 61 | 67 | +7 |
| OTC medications | N/A | 19 | N/A |

Source: WSL Marketing Inc., 2005

## 1. Keywords for Holiday Advertising

To get your holiday advertising season rolling, we have compiled a list of popular keywords during each holiday season (yes, we consider the Super Bowl a holiday). Use these keywords to increase traffic to your site, but make sure they are relevant to the products being offered. Since Google allows you to advertise to hundreds of foreign countries, various holidays from around the world are shown.

### FOLLOW THE ONE MONTH ADVERTISING RULE

Set holiday advertising campaigns to begin one month prior to the holiday (Christmas being a big exception) when most of the purchasing is done. Set the date your holiday campaign will start when creating a new campaign under the "Set Pricing" section and you can set the end date under the "Edit Campaign Settings" section.

## a. New Year's

| Date | Country |
|------|---------|
| January 1$^{st}$ | Most Countries |
| January 21$^{st}$-February 21$^{st}$ (1$^{st}$ Winter New Moon) | China, Vietnam |
| April 13$^{th}$-April 15$^{th}$ | Thailand |

## Popular New Year's Search Terms

Air Pumps
Balloons
Bottle Rockets
Bowties
Champaign
Champaign Glasses
Chinese Dragons
Cigars
Cocktail Dresses
Confetti
Cuban Cigars
Cufflinks
Diamond Bracelets
Diamond Necklaces
Diamond Rings
Dinner Dresses
Disco Balls
Dominican Cigars
Firecrackers
Fireworks
Formal Attire

Formal Wear
Gold Bracelets
Gold Necklaces
Gold Pendants
Gold Rings
Honduran Cigars
Leather Overcoats
Leather Pumps
Limos
Limousines
Long Stemmed Glasses
Long Stemmed Roses
Nail Polish
New Year's Catering
New Year's Event Planning
Overcoats
Paper Dragons
Party Favors
Party Hats

Party Recipes
Party Trays
Patent Leather Pumps
Patent Leather Shoes
Pumps
Rental Limousines
Rental Tuxedos
Roses
Serving Platters
Silver Bracelets
Silver Necklaces
Silver Pendants
Silver Rings
Sparklers
Stretch Limos
Times Square
Tennis Bracelets
Tuxedos
Wine

## b. Super Bowl

| Date | Country |
|------|---------|
| January 28th | United States |

## Popular Super Bowl Search Terms

Armchairs
Bean Bags
Bean Bag Chairs
Bean Dip
Bean Dip Recipes
Big Screen TVs
Big Screen Televisions
Chip Dip Recipes
Condiments
Digital Video Recorders
Dip Recipes
DVRs
Flat Panel TVs
Flat Panel Televisions
Flat Panel Mounts
Flat Panel Wall Mounts
Flat Screen TVs
Flat Screen Televisions

Flat Screen Mounts
Flat Screen Wall Mounts
Footballs
Football Cakes
Football Cupcakes
HD TVs
HD Televisions
LCD TVs
LCD Televisions
Leather Recliners
NFL Footballs
NFL Jerseys
Party Favors
Party Recipes
Party Trays
Plasma TVs
Plasma Televisions
Recliners
Serving Platters
Serving Trays
Super Bowl Cakes
Super Bowl Catering

Super Bowl Hats
Super Bowl Jerseys
Super Bowl Recipes
Super Bowl Shirts
Super Bowl T Shirts
Super Bowl Tee Shirts
Surround Sound Receivers
Surround Sound Speakers
Surround Sound Systems
Television Mounts
Television Wall Mounts
TV Mounts
TV Trays
TV Wall Mounts
Widescreen Televisions
Widescreen TVs

## c. Valentine's Day

| Date | Country |
|------|---------|
| February 14th | Europe, Japan, Korea, United States |
| March 14th | Japan and Korea (White Day) |
| June 12th | Brazil (Boyfriend's/Girlfriend's Day) |
| March 21st | Egypt, Lebanon, Syria, Jordan |
| 7th Day of 7th Month of Lunar Calendar | China (The Night of Sevens) |

## Popular Valentine's Day Search Terms

Belgian Chocolate
Best Chocolate
Candy Flowers
Candy Gift Boxes
Candy Hearts
Cheap Roses
Chocolate Flowers
Chocolate Gift Boxes
Chocolate Hearts
Cupid Dolls
Cupid Photos
Dark Chocolate
Dozen Roses
Diamonds
Diamond Bracelets
Diamond Earrings
Diamond Necklaces
Diamonds Online
Diamond Pendants
Diamond Rings
Dinner Dresses
Engagement Ring
European Chocolate
Fine Chocolate

Gold Bracelets
Gold Lockets
Gold Necklaces
Gold Pendants
Gold Rings
Gourmet Candy
Gourmet Chocolate
Heart Jewelry
Fine Chocolate
Fine Dark Chocolate
Flower Bouquet
Flower Delivery
Long Stemmed Roses
Love Poems
Massage Card
Massage Oil
Milk Chocolate
Organic Chocolate
Premium Chocolate
Promise Ring
Red Dresses
Romantic Recipes
Romantic Gifts
Romantic Gift Ideas

Romantic Poems
Roses
Roses Delivery
Sterling Silver
Silver Bracelets
Silver Jewelry
Silver Lockets
Silver Necklaces
Silver Pendants
Silver Rings
Spa Gift Certificates
Spa Trips
Valentine Bouquet
Valentine Cards
Valentine Day Roses
Valentine E-cards
Valentine Flowers
Valentine Gifts
Valentine Gift Ideas
Valentine Roses
White Chocolate

## d. St. Patrick's Day

| Date | Country |
|------|---------|
| March 17th | Australia, Austria, Belgium, Brazil, Canada, China, Denmark, Finland, Germany, Hong Kong, Ireland, Italy, Japan, Korea, the Netherlands, New Zealand, Peru, Russia, Singapore, Slovakia, South Africa, United Kingdom, United States |

## Popular St. Patrick's Day Search Terms

Blarney Stone
Baseball Caps
Blarney Stone
Baseball Hats
Blarney Stone Hats
Blarney Stone Tee
Shirts
Blarney Stone T-
Shirts
Books on Ireland
Food Coloring
Four Leaf Clovers
Green Face Paint
Green Food Coloring
Green Ties
Green Tights
Irish Authors
Irish Folklore Books
Irish Legend Books
Irish Music
Irish Musicians
"Kiss Me I'm Irish"
Baseball Caps
"Kiss Me I'm Irish"
Baseball Hats

"Kiss Me I'm Irish"
Hats
"Kiss Me I'm Irish"
Tee Shirts
"Kiss Me I'm Irish"
T-Shirts
Leprechaun Baseball
Caps
Leprechaun Baseball
Hats
Leprechaun
Costumes
Leprechaun Hats
Leprechaun Tee
Shirts
Leprechaun T-Shirts
"Luck of the Irish"
Baseball Caps
"Luck of the Irish"
Baseball Hats
"Luck of the Irish"
Hats
"Luck of the Irish"
Tee Shirts
"Luck of the Irish" T-

Shirts
"Luck O' the Irish"
Baseball Caps
"Luck O' the Irish"
Baseball Hats
"Luck O' the Irish"
Hats
"Luck O' the Irish"
Tee Shirts
"Luck O' the Irish"
T-Shirts
Shamrock Baseball
Caps
Shamrock Baseball
Hats
Shamrock Hats
Shamrock Tee Shirts
Shamrock T-Shirts
St. Patrick's Day
Gifts
St. Patrick's Day Gift
Ideas
St. Patrick's Day
Recipes

## e. Easter

| Date | Country |
|------|---------|
| Sunday Between March 22-April 25 | Albania, Argentina, Australia, Austria, Belgium, Brazil, Canada, Chile, Costa Rica, Denmark, Dominican Republic, Estonia, Finland, France, Germany, Hungary, Ireland, Italy, Latvia, Lithuania, Malta, Mexico, Netherlands, New Zealand, Norway, Peru, Poland, Portugal, Singapore, Slovakia, South Africa, Spain, Sweden, United Kingdom, United States |

## Popular Easter Search Terms

Bibles
Candy Eggs
Chocolate Bunnies
Chocolate Easter Egg Candy
Chocolate Eggs
Chocolate Rabbits
Crucifixes
Wall Crucifixes
Easter Baskets
Easter Basket Candy
Easter Basket Grass
Easter Bunny Costumes
Easter Candy
Easter Egg Coloring Kits
Easter Egg Decorating Kits
Easter Gifts
Easter Gift Ideas
Easter Keepsakes
Easter Lilies
Easter Recipes
Easter Toys
Egg Decorating Kits
Egg Food Coloring
Food Coloring
King James Bibles
NIV Bibles
Rosary
"The Passion of the Christ"
"The Passion of the Christ" DVD
"The Passion of the Christ" Movie
"The Passion of the Christ" Video
Tulip Bulbs

## f. Mother's Day

| Date | Country |
|------|---------|
| 2nd Sunday in February | Norway |
| 4th Sunday in Lent | Ireland, United Kingdom |
| March 21st | Egypt, Lebanon, Syria, Jordan |
| 1st Sunday in May | Hungary, Lithuania, Portugal, South Africa, Spain |
| May 8th | South Korea (Parent's Day) |
| May 10th | Bahrain, Chile, India, Malaysia, Mexico, Oman, Pakistan, Qatar, Saudi Arabia, United Arab Emirates |
| 2nd Sunday in May | Australia, Austria, Belgium, Brazil, Canada, China, Denmark, Estonia, Finland, Germany, Hong Kong, Italy, Japan, Latvia, Malta, the Netherlands, New Zealand, Peru, Singapore, Slovakia, Taiwan, Turkey, United States |
| May 26th | Poland |
| Last Sunday in May | Sweden, Dominican Republic |
| 1st Sunday in June or Last Sunday in May | France |
| August 12th | Thailand (Birthday of Queen Sirikit Kitiyakara) |
| August 15th | Belgium, Costa Rica |
| 2nd or 3rd Sunday in October | Argentina |
| November 28th | Russia |
| December 8th | Panama |

## Popular Mother's Day Search Terms

Flower Bouquet Delivery
Flower Delivery
Internet Flowers
Internet Flower Bouquet Delivery
Internet Flower Delivery
Massage Gift Certificates
Mother's Day Cards
Mother's Day Flowers
Mother's Day Gifts
Mother's Day Gift Certificates

Mother's Day Gift Ideas
Mother's Day Keepsakes
Online Flowers
Online Flower Bouquets
Picture Frames
Photo Albums
Restaurant Gift Certificates
Roses Delivery
Scrapbooks
Spa Gift Certificate

## g. Father's Day

| Date | Country |
|------|---------|
| February 23$^{rd}$ | Russia (Army Day) |
| March 19$^{th}$ | Italy (St. Joseph's Day), Spain, Portugal |
| May 5$^{th}$ | Germany (Ascension Day) |
| May 8$^{th}$ | South Korea (Parents' Day) |
| June 5$^{th}$ | Denmark (Also Constitution Day) |
| 1$^{st}$ Sunday in June | Lithuania |
| 2$^{nd}$ Sunday in June | Austria, Belgium (Secular) |
| June 20$^{th}$ | Bulgaria |
| 3$^{rd}$ Sunday in June | Argentina, Canada, Chile, France, Hong Kong, India, Japan, Macao, Malta, Mexico, Netherlands, Slovakia, Turkey, United Kingdom, United States, Peru, Venezuela |
| 3$^{rd}$ Week in June | Malaysia |
| June 23$^{rd}$ | Poland |
| August 8$^{th}$ | Taiwan |
| 2$^{nd}$ Sunday in August | Brazil |
| 1$^{st}$ Sunday in September | Australia, New Zealand |
| 2$^{nd}$ Sunday in November | Finland, Norway, Sweden |
| December 5$^{th}$ | Thailand |

## Popular Father's Day Search Terms

Discount Golf Bags
Discount Golf Clubs
Discount Golf Equipment
Discount Golf Gloves
Discount Golf Hats
Discount Golf Shoes
Discount Golfing
Discount Tools
Electronics Store Gift Certificates
Golf Balls
Golf Clubs
Golf Gift Certificates

Golf Gloves
Golf Hats
Golf Shoes
Internet Flowers
Internet Flower
Bouquet Delivery
Internet Flower Delivery
Father's Day Cards
Father's Day Gifts
Father's Day Gift Ideas
Father's Day Gift Certificates

Father's Day Tools
Motorcycle Gear
Neckties
Online Flowers
Online Flower
Bouquets
Picture Frames
Photo Albums
Restaurant Gift Certificates
Sports Books
Sports Movies
Ties

### h. Memorial Day

| Date | Country |
|---|---|
| Last Monday in May | United States |

## MEMORIAL DAY IS UNIQUE TO THE UNITED STATES

The United States is the only country that commemorates people who *died* in military service. The United States, along with most European countries, observe Veteran's Day/Remembrance on November 11th to honor those in military service who *survived*. May 8th is France's World War II Victory Day.

## Popular Memorial Day Search Terms

Armchairs
Bean Bags
Bean Bag Chairs
Bean Dip
Bean Dip Recipes
Big Screen TVs
Big Screen
Televisions
Chip Dip Recipes
Condiments
Digital Video
Recorders
Dip Recipes
Fishing Bait

Fishing Boats
Fishing Line
Fishing Lures
Fishing Rods
Fishing Tackle Boxes
Flag Pins
Folding Chairs
Grave Markers
Internet Flowers
Internet Flower
Bouquet Delivery
Internet Flower
Delivery
Keepsake Boxes

Keepsake Chests
Miniature Flags
Online Flowers
Online Flower
Bouquets
Party Favors
Party Recipes
Party Trays
Photo Albums
Recliners
Serving Platters
Serving Trays

## i. Independence Day

| Date | Country |
|------|---------|
| May 8th | France (World War II Victory Day) |
| June 5th | Denmark (Constitution Day and Father's Day) |
| July 4th | United States |

## Popular Independence Day Search Terms

American Flags
Armchairs
Barbecue Grills
Barbecue Grill Tools
Barbecue Grill Utensils
Barbeque Recipes
Barbecue Ribs
Barbecue Sauce
Bean Dip
Bean Dip Recipes
Blankets
Bug Spray
Bug Spray with Deet
Chip Dip Recipes
Collapsible Chairs
Collapsible Tables
Condiments
Declaration of Independence
Dip Recipes
Firecrackers
Fireworks
Fishing Bait
Fishing Boats
Fishing Line
Fishing Lures
Fishing Rods
Fishing Tackle Boxes

Folding Chairs
Founding Fathers
Fourth of July Recipes
Grilling Tools
Grilling Utensils
Hamburger Buns
Hamburger Recipes
Hamburger Buns
Hamburger Recipes
Inner Tubes
Mosquito Lotion
Mosquito Spray
Outdoor Grills
Outdoor Smokers
Party Favors
Party Recipes
Party Trays
Patio Furniture
Patio Tables
Patriotic Baseball Hats
Patriotic Hats
Patriotic Shirts
Patriotic Table Cloths
Patriotic T-Shirts
Patriotic Tee Shirts
Photo Albums
Potato Salad Recipes

Red, White and Blue Baseball Hats
Red, White and Blue Cakes
Red, White and Blue Cupcakes
Red, White and Blue Hats
Red, White and Blue Headbands
Red, White and Blue Shirts
Red, White and Blue Table Cloths
Red, White and Blue T-Shirts
Red, White and Blue Tee Shirts
Recliners
Serving Platters
Serving Trays
Sparklers
Sun Block
Suntan Lotion
Tackle Boxes
US Flags
Water Crafts
Water Skis

## j. Labor Day

| Date | Country |
|------|---------|
| 1st Monday in March | Western Australia |
| 2nd Monday in March | Tasmania, Australia (Eight Hours Day); Victoria, Australia |
| May 1st | Europe (May Day); Poland (State Holiday) |
| 1st Monday in May | Queensland, Australia; Northern Territory (May Day) |
| 1st Monday in September | Canada, United States |
| 1st Monday in October | Australian Capital Territory; New South Wales, Australia; South Australia |
| 4th Monday in October | New Zealand |

## AUSTRALIA VARIES DATE OF LABOR DAY BY STATE/TERRITORY

Australia has four different days for Labor Day depending upon the particular state/territory. Google allows local advertising in Australia, so you must fine-tune your campaign to address this discrepancy unlike all other countries where you can focus your campaign at the country level for most holidays. Visit www.Google.com.au for more information.

## Popular Labor Day Search Terms

Armchairs
Barbecue Grills
Barbecue Grill Tools
Barbecue Grill Utensils
Barbeque Recipes
Barbecue Ribs
Barbecue Sauce
Bean Dip
Bean Dip Recipes
Blankets
Bug Spray
Bug Spray with Deet

Chip Dip Recipes
Collapsible Chairs
Collapsible Tables
Condiments
Dip Recipes
Fishing Bait
Fishing Boats
Fishing Line
Fishing Lures
Fishing Rods
Fishing Tackle Boxes
Folding Chairs

Grilling Tools
Grilling Utensils
Hamburger Buns
Hamburger Recipes
Hamburger Buns
Hamburger Recipes
Inner Tubes
Mosquito Lotion
Mosquito Spray
Outdoor Grills
Outdoor Smokers
Party Favors
Party Recipes

Party Trays
Patio Furniture
Patio Tables
Picnic Baskets
Potato Salad Recipes
Recliners
Serving Platters
Serving Trays
Sun Block
Suntan Lotion
Tackle Boxes
Water Crafts
Water Skis

## k. Halloween

| Date | Country |
|---|---|
| October 31$^{st}$ | Australia, Canada, Ireland, New Zealand, Puerto Rico, United Kingdom, United States |
| 2$^{nd}$ Monday in March | Tasmania, Australia (Eight Hours Day); Victoria, Australia |
| May 1$^{st}$ | Europe (May Day); Poland (State Holiday) |
| 1$^{st}$ Monday in May | Queensland, Australia; Northern Territory (May Day) |
| 1$^{st}$ Monday in September | |
| 1$^{st}$ Monday in October | Australian Capital Territory; New South Wales, Australia; South Australia |
| 4$^{th}$ Monday in October | New Zealand |

## Popular Halloween Search Terms

Apple Cider
Apple Cider Recipes
Apple Cider Spices
Barmbrack
Bats
Black Cats
Candy Apples
Candy Apple Carmel Wrappers
Candy Apple Recipes
Candy Bags
Candy Corn
Carmel Apples
Carmel Apple Recipes
Devil Costumes
Dracula Capes
Dracula Costumes
Dracula Masks
Dracula Teeth
Face Paint
Frankenstein Costumes

Frankenstein Masks
Ghost Costumes
Ghost Outfits
Ghost Masks
Goblin Costumes
Goblin Masks
Goblin Outfits
Halloween Baskets
Halloween Cakes
Halloween Caldrons
Halloween Candy
Halloween Costumes
Halloween Cupcakes
Halloween Gags
Halloween Jack O' Lanterns
Halloween Masks
Halloween Recipes
Halloween Tricks
Jack O' Lanterns
Kobold Ausstattung
Kobold Kostüm
Kobold Schablone

Leaf Rakes
Legend of Sleepy Hollow
Mummy Costumes
Pirate Costumes
Plastic Bats
Plastic Jack O' Lanterns
Plastic Pumpkins
Plastic Spiders
Political Figure Costumes
Political Figure Masks
President Masks
Princess Costumes
Pumpkins
Pumpkin Carving
Pumpkin Carving Knives
Pumpkin Carving Tools
Pumpkin Leaf Bags

Pumpkin Pie
Pumpkin Pie Recipes
Pumpkin Recipes
Pumpkin Seeds
Pumpkin Seed
Recipes
Rubber Bats
Rubber Spiders
Satan Costumes
Scary Costumes
Scary Music
Scary Wigs
Skeletons

Skeleton Costumes
Skeleton Masks
Skeleton Outfits
Trick or Treat
Baskets
Trick or Treat Cakes
Trick or Treat
Caldrons
Trick or Treat Candy
Trick or Treat
Costumes
Trick or Treat
Cupcakes

Trick or Treat Jack
O' Lanterns
Trick or Treat Masks
Trick or Treat
Recipes
Werewolf Costumes
Werewolf Masks
Witch Costumes
Witch Fingers
Witch Masks
Witch Noses
Zombies
Zombie Masks

## COST-PER-CLICK & BIDDING MISPERCEPTION

It is a common misperception when you are the only one bidding on a certain holiday keyword (or any keyword at all) that you can bid $0.01 per click and that will be your minimum bid. The Quality Score determines the minimum CPC. If you do not have high quality ads, your minimum CPC will continue to rise even if no one is bidding against you. If your ad is the only one showing for a keyword, you should have a high CTR and your Quality Score should improve accordingly, thus lowering your minimum CPC over time.

## 1. All Saint's Day

| Date | Country |
|---|---|
| November 1$^{st}$ | Ireland, France, Germany, Mexico, Philippines, Poland, Portugal, Scotland, Spain, United Kingdom |
| 1$^{st}$ Saturday in November | Switzerland |

### Popular All Saint's Day Search Terms

Armchairs
Blankets
Candles
Charcoal
Coolers
Flowers
Flower Wreathes
Folding Chairs
Grave Markers

Gills
Lighter Fluid
Party Favors
Party Recipes
Party Trays
Picnic Baskets
Umbrellas
Votives

## m. All Soul's Day

| Date | Country |
|------|---------|
| November $2^{nd}$ | Brazil, Mexico, Philippines |

## Popular All Soul's Day Search Terms

Bread of the Dead (*Pan de Muerto*)
Candles (*Velas*)
Flower of the Dead (*Flor de Muerto*)
Flowers (*Flors*)
Flower Wreathes (*La Flor Wreathes*)
Grave Markers (*Marcadores Graves*)
Little Angels (*Los Angelitos*)
Orange Marigolds (*Maravillas Anaranjadas*)
Short Poems (*Calaveras*)
Skeletons (*Calacas*)
Skeleton Costumes (*Calaca Trajes*)
Skeleton Masks (*Calacas Máscaras*)
Skulls (*Calaveras*)
Skull Masks (*Calaveras Máscaras*)
Sugar Skulls (Azúcar Calaveras)
Twenty Flower (*Cempazúchil*)
Votives (*Votives*)

## n. Thanksgiving

| Date | Country |
|------|---------|
| August 15th | Poland (Dozynki) |
| Mid-September – 1st Week of October | Germany (Oktoberfest) |
| 2nd Monday in October | Canada |
| 4th Thursday in November | United States |

## Popular Thanksgiving Day Search Terms

Candied Walnuts
Canola Oil
Cajun Turkeys
Floats
Free Range Turkeys
Fried Turkeys
Fried Turkey Oil
Grain Fed Turkeys
Gravy
Gravy Recipes
Green Bean
Casserole
Green Bean
Casserole Recipes
Ham
Ham Recipes
Honey Glazed Ham
Honey Roasted Ham
Recipes

Internet Turkeys
Mail Order
Thanksgiving Meals
Mail Order Turkeys
Mashed Potatoes
Mashed Potato
Meat Thermometer
Recipes
Mayflower
Online Turkeys
Peanut Oil
Pilgrims
Pumpkin Leaf Bags
Pumpkin Pie
Pumpkin Pie Recipes
Roasted Turkeys
Smoked Turkeys
Stuffing Recipes
Sweet Potatoes

Sweet Potato Recipes
Thanksgiving Gift
Ideas
Thanksgiving Day
Parades
Turkey Bags
Turkey Basters
Turkey Cookers
Turkey Oven Bags
Turkey Oven
Thermometers
Turkey Recipes
Turkey Stuffing
Turkey Temperature
Thermometers
Turkey Vats
Yams
Yam Recipes

## BLACK FRIDAY & CYBER MONDAY

"Black Friday" is the day after Thanksgiving in the U.S. and is typically the busiest shopping day of the year. "Cyber Monday" is the Monday *after* Thanksgiving and the busiest online shopping day of the year as people return to work and their *computers*. Ensure your ads are getting their max impressions on this day.

## o. Christmas

| Date | Country |
|---|---|
| December 25th | Most Countries Apart from Jewish and Islamic States |

## Popular Christmas Search Terms

A Christmas Carol
A Christmas Carol Play
Airline Gift Certificates
Artificial Christmas Trees
Babes in Toyland
Best Fruitcakes
Bethlehem
Birth of Christ
Books About Jesus Birth
Books About Santa
Candied Walnuts
Candle Light Services
Candy Canes
Charles Dickens
Christmas Bows
Christmas Cards
Christmas Dresses
Christmas Eve Services
Christmas Gift Cards
Christmas Gift Certificates
Christmas Gifts for a Boyfriend
Christmas Gifts for a Child

Christmas Gifts for a Girlfriend
Christmas Gifts for a Husband
Christmas Gifts for a Man
Christmas Gifts for a Toddler
Christmas Gifts for a Wife
Christmas Gifts for a Woman
Christmas Gifts Under $10
Christmas Gifts Under $20
Christmas Jazz
Christmas Jazz Music
Christmas Light Installers
Christmas Music
Christmas Rock
Christmas Rock Music
Christmas Services
Christmas Stockings
Christmas Stocking Stuffer Ideas
Christmas String
Christmas Traditions
Christmas Trees

Christmas Tree Bags
Christmas Tree Garland
Christmas Tree Icicles
Christmas Tree Lights
Christmas Tree Ornaments
Christmas Tree Stands
Christmas Tunes
Christmas Wrapping Paper
Christmas Wreaths
Discount Bows
Discount Christmas Bows
Discount Christmas Cards
Discount Christmas Wrapping Paper
Discount Gift Cards
Discount Wrapping Paper
Favorite Christmas Songs
Fiber Optic Christmas Trees
Frosty the Snowman
Frosty the Snowman

DVDs
Frosty the Snowman Movies
Fruitcakes
Gas Gift Cards
Giant Candy Canes
Gift Baskets
Gift Ideas for a Boyfriend
Gift Ideas for a Child
Gift Ideas for a Girlfriend
Gift Ideas for a Husband
Gift Ideas for a Man
Gift Ideas for a Toddler
Gift Ideas for a Wife
Gift Ideas for a Woman
Gingerbread Cookies
Gingerbread Cookie Recipes
Gingerbread House
Gingerbread Recipes
Handmade Christmas Gifts
Handmade Christmas Tree Ornaments
Herb Wreath
History of Santa
Holiday Gift Card
Holiday Gift Certificate
Holiday Gifts for a Boyfriend
Holiday Gifts for a Child
Holiday Gifts for a Girlfriend

Holiday Gifts for a Husband
Holiday Gifts for a Man
Holiday Gifts for a Toddler
Holiday Gifts for a Wife
Holiday Gifts for a Woman
Holiday Gifts Under $10
Holiday Gifts Under $20
Hot Children's Christmas Toys
Hot Children's Toys
Hot Christmas Toys
Last Minute Christmas Gifts
Lighted Wreath
Live Christmas Trees
Mary and Joseph
Manger
Manger Scenes
Massage Gift Certificates
Meat Thermometer
Mistletoe
Movie Gift Certificates
North Pole
Nut Cracker
Nut Cracker Suite
Outdoor Christmas Garland
Outdoor Christmas Lights
Outdoor Garland
Outdoor Lights

Pre-lit Wreaths
Popular Children's Christmas Toys
Popular Children's Toys
Popular Christmas Songs
Popular Christmas Toys
Popular Gifts for Men
Popular Gifts for Women
Pre-Lit Christmas Trees
Present Ideas
Real Christmas Garland
Real Christmas Trees
Real Christmas Wreathes
Real Garland
Real Wreathes
Restaurant Gift Certificates
Romantic Christmas Gifts
Romantic Holiday Gifts
Santa
Santa Clause
Santa's Workshop
Secret Santa Gifts
Spa Gift Certificates
Stocking Coal
Stocking Stuffers
Stocking Stuffer Ideas
The Story of Christmas
Toy Trains

Toy Train Sets
Toy Train Tracks
Traditional Christmas
Songs
Train Sets
Travel Gift
Certificates
Turkey Bags

Turkey Basters
Turkey Oven Bags
Turkey Oven
Thermometers
Turkey Recipes
Turkey Temperature
Thermometers
Turkey Stuffing

Wrapping Paper
Wreath Hanger
Wreath Storage Bags
Wreath Storage
Boxes
Yams
Yam Recipes

## CHRISTMAS IS THE ONE MONTH ADVERTISING RULE EXCEPTION

We discussed above that you should set your holiday advertising campaign to begin one month prior to the holiday when most of the purchasing is done. The exception is Christmas. The holiday shopping season begins the middle of October. If your Christmas campaign is not started by October 15$^{th}$ you are losing potential Christmas sales.

### p. Boxing Day

| Date | Country |
|---|---|
| December 26th | Belgium, Catalonia (St. Stephen's Day), Denmark, France, Germany, Ireland (St. Stephen's Day), Italy, Netherlands, Norway, South Africa (Day of Goodwill), Sweden, Wales (St. Stephen's Day) |
| 1st Weekday After Christmas | Australia, Canada, New Zealand, United Kingdom |

## Popular Boxing Day Search Terms

Boxing Day Gift Certificates
Boxing Day Gift Ideas
Cricket Equipment
Cricket Gear
Fishing Boats
Footballs
Football Gear
Football Jerseys
Football Shoes
Football Shorts

Horse Racing
Picnic Baskets
Picnic Utensils
Soccer Balls
Soccer Gear
Soccer Jerseys
Soccer Shoes
Soccer Shorts
Wickets
Yacht Racing

## 2. Holiday Strategies

After the holidays, once you have disabled your advertising campaign, the Google team makes it easy to resume it the next year. All you have to do is select the disabled campaign and resume it. Be mindful, however, of the dates you have selected for the campaign to run, especially for holidays that are on different days each year such as Easter.

### THE BUSIEST SHOPPING DAY OF THE YEAR

December 14th is the busiest shopping day of the year and sales taper off until January, which is the slowest month of shopping for most businesses. But the recent popularity of gift cards makes the last week of December and first two weeks of January also busier than normal shopping times.

Keep sufficient inventory on hand for increased sales during the holiday season. There is nothing that will turn off a customer faster than a season gift not delivered on time for the holidays.

### FOCUS ON YOUR HOLIDAY LANDING PAGES

It is sometimes easy to forget to change the landing pages linked to your holiday ads. Holiday shoppers want to see landing pages that are tailored to the seasonal item they are searching for. If they view a Christmas ad in January, that will be a turn off.

## V. Image Ads
In 2004 Google announced the availability of Image Ads for its AdWord customers. This came as a surprise to many in the Internet world given Google's previous distaste for graphic advertising. Now Google has extended Image Ads to include movement.

### A. Static Ads
Static ads are the traditional Google Image Ads. The ads can be uploaded to Google in the following formats:
- .JPG (Static Graphic)
- .GIF (Static Graphic)
- .PNG (Static Graphic)

Google does not show Image Ads on its Website or within the Search Network.

### 1. Static Ad Sizes
Of the eleven square and rectangle sizes in which AdSense ads are displayed, Image Ads may only be created in five sizes:

| Image Ad Formats |
| --- |
| • Medium Rectangle [Vertical Rectangle] (300x250) |
| • Banner [Horizontal Rectangle] (468x60) |
| • Skyscraper [Vertical Rectangle] (120x600) |
| • Wide Skyscraper [Vertical Rectangle] (160 X 600) |
| • Leaderboard [Horizontal Rectangle] (728x90) |

## Medium Rectangle (300 x 250)

## Leaderboard (728 x 90)

## Banner (468 x 60)

**Skyscraper (120 x 600)**

**Wide Skyscraper (160 x 600)**

At the appropriate place within each static Image Ad Google will place a line that provides your URL (or affiliate's URL if you are redirecting for another Website) and the statement "Feedback - Ads by Google." Google will actually resize your images to accommodate this line. We recommend resizing the image yourself since it gives you more control over the content. If you want to prevent resizing by leaving space for Google, here are the smaller sizes you must upload.

---

### Reduced Static Ad Formats

- Leaderboard [Horizontal Rectangle] (728x79)
- Banner [Horizontal Rectangle] (468x49)
- Skyscraper [Vertical Rectangle] (120x578)
- Wide Skyscraper [Vertical Rectangle] (160 X 578)
- Medium Rectangle [Vertical Rectangle] (300x239)

---

## MULTIPLE IMAGE ADS PER GROUP

Multiple Image Ads may be created per Ad Group so try a variation and see which are getting you the most clicks.

Image ads, given their size, displace a number of AdWords textual advertisements on each site. Therefore, the major downside to running an Image Ad campaign is that your ad must receive two to five times as many clicks as a text ad to get impressions shown. For example, the Wide Skyscraper ads take the place of *five* text ads down one column of the screen. This is the only Image Ad size that replaces five text ads, which means that your Skyscraper Image Ad must be getting more clicks than *all* of the five text ads it is replacing combined!

## EDITORIAL GUIDELINES SIMILAR TO TEXT ADS

Only "family safe" images are allowed on Image Ads and the images must not be misleading as to the product/service being sold or act like Windows/Mac error boxes. Competitive claims and product discounts or "free" ads must be supported on the Website landing page. Adhere to Google's trademark usage guidelines: http://www.google.com/permissions/trademarks.html

## 2. Static Ad Style Guidelines

Static ads have the ability to draw even more user attention, and therefore more clicks, than text ads. If they are not done correctly, however, they have the potential of ruining your advertising campaign. Acutely aware of this, Google has set forth a number of static ad style guidelines.

### Static Ad Style Guidelines

- Text ads may not be mimicked (i.e., you may not make your Image Ad look like it is a block of text ads).
- Ad must occupy entire space of ad block.
- Prizes may not be offered for clicking on the ad.
- Ads cannot be sideways in the ad space or upside down.
- Ads must not extend out of the ad space allotted.
- Ads may not be divided to appear like two or more ads.

## EXPANDED TEXT ADS?

Google is now testing expanded text ads that will take up the entire space of a normal ad unit. Look for these in the near future.

### B. Animated Ads

At first Google did not allow Image Ads to move, but that has all changed. Image ads can move if desired. Google calls these animated ads. Contrary to popular belief, Google allows flash ads to be included as Image Ads. The ads can be uploaded to Google in the following formats:

- .GIF (Animated Graphic)
- .SWF (Animated Graphic)

## FILE SIZE LIMITS

Animated file sizes are limited to 50 Kilobytes.

### 1. Flash Ads

Flash ads are unique types of animated ads that are uploaded in the same manner as other graphic files, but must be formatted in flash versions 4-6. Flash ads must also support clickTAG. This is the tracking code Google will assign to your flash ad to track where it is advertised and the number of clicks. Redirection in the ad when clicked upon must be sent to the URL listed in the clickTAG only. The variable name must be exactly spelled "clickTAG" here is the code:

```
on (release){
if (clickTAG.substr(0,5)=="http:"){
get URL(clickTAG, "_top");
}
}
```

## FLASH AD EDITORIAL GUIDELINES

The same editorial guidelines that apply to other Image Ads also apply to flash ads. Please visit https://adwords.google.com/select/imageguidelines.html for Google's latest guidelines.

## 2. Animated Ad Style Guidelines

Animated ads have the ability to draw even more user attention, and therefore more clicks, than static ads. If they are not done correctly, however, they have the potential of ruining your advertising campaign. Acutely aware of this, Google has set forth a number of strict animated ad style guidelines.

### Animated Ad Style Guidelines

- Animated ads cannot flash or strobe. *Thanks Google!*
- Ads that simulate computer functions ("Trick-to-Click") are not allowed.
- Prizes may not be offered for clicking on the ad.
- No looping animation is allowed. All animation must be finished within 30 seconds of the ad being displayed.
- Ads must not extend out of the ad space allotted.

## C. Image Ad Advertising Space

### 1. Physical Space

Image Ads grab the attention of users quicker than text ads and, in turn, animated Image Ads grab the attention of users quicker than static ads. The downside is the greater number of clicks Image Ads must receive (more than *all* of the text ads it is replacing) and the ability of Content Network owners to select between running just text ads or both text and Image Ads.

## DRIVE OUT FIVE COMPETITORS WITH IMAGE ADS

> Run Wide Skyscraper Image Ads to replace five text ads of your competitors. Ensure that you will get more clicks than any of the text ads. What a great way to drive out the competition in droves!

Google requires your Image Ad to have relevance to your keywords. If you have selected rakes, shovels, and hoes as your keywords, you must show garden tools in your image ad.

## RUN BOTH IMAGE ADS AND ADWORDS

> Run both Image Ads and text ads for your marketing campaign so your advertising is assured broad coverage. Google does not allow AdSense Websites to display only Image Ads on a page. They have the option to either have text only ads or a combination of text and graphical ads on a page. This allows Google to channel only the most relevant, click-worthy ads to your Website.

## 2. Effective Cost Per Impression

We've established that since Image Ads displace an entire unit of text ads, Google requires them to operate at higher click rates. If they do not perform well, Google's computer algorithms will yank the Image Ads and put the text ads back in place. Google uses what's called an effective Cost Per Impression (eCPM) model to compare Image Ads and textual ads.

$$eCMP = 1000 \ x \ \frac{\text{Total Earnings}}{\text{Impressions}}$$

For instance, if your total earnings are $1 for 100 impressions, your eCMP=($0.01)(1000) or $10. This means you should make $10 for each 1000 impressions.

Google ensures that CPM ads on the Content Network site will yield the highest eCMP, regardless of whether they are Image Ads or text ads. Let's compare the number of text ads the five Image Ad sizes displace and the resulting eCPM.

| Image Ad Formats | Number of Text Ads Displaced | Effective Cost Per Impression |
|---|---|---|
| Banner (468X60) (28,080 Total Area) | Two | $\frac{(CPC)(CTR)}{2}$ |
| Leaderboard (728X90) (65,520 Total Area) | Four | $\frac{(CPC)(CTR)}{4}$ |
| Medium Rectangle (300x250) (75,000 Total Area) | Four | $\frac{(CPC)(CTR)}{4}$ |
| Skyscraper (120x600) (72,000 Total Area) | Four | $\frac{(CPC)(CTR)}{4}$ |
| Wide Skyscraper (160 X 600) (96,000 Total Area) | Five | $\frac{(CPC)(CTR)}{5}$ |

What this tells us is that Banner Image Ads must have twice the eCPM of the combination of two text ads it replaces. The Leaderboard, Medium Rectangle, and Skyscraper must have four times the eCPM of the four text ads they replace and the Wide Skyscraper must have five times the eCPM for it to be shown over the five text ads it displaces.

From a pure analysis of Image Ad area versus the number of text ads displaced, the Medium Rectangle and Wide Skyscraper are the best footprint value. This is no coincidence; per Google, the Medium Rectangle and Wide Skyscraper are the *two best* performing Image Ads. Focus your Image Ad campaign using these formats and you off to gaining more clicks and excluding the competition.

## SMART PRICING APPLIES TO IMAGE ADS

Google's Smart Pricing feature applies to Image Ads so that if Google determines that clicks are less likely to convert on a Content Network site, the CPC will automatically be reduced.

### D. Image Ad Colors

The colors you pick for your Image Ads are vitally important to their success. They are no less significant than text for AdWords. Remember also, that limited text can be used in your Image Ads. Strive to adopt the same attention-getting principles used throughout this book for Image Ad text. Following are tips for getting your Image Ad noticed and for avoiding confusing tone combinations.

### 1. Foreground vs. Background Contrasts

Using a light background color with dark text is the preferred method of viewing Image Ads on the Internet. This way the text jumps off the page at searchers. This is the same technique Web designers have used since the mid-nineties.

## BE CAREFUL OF BORDER COLORS

Ensure the tones of your ad work well in multiple border colors. AdSense Websites can change the border colors of Image Ads.

If no text in the Image Ad, make key images dark with a pale background.

### AVOID CLOSELY-RELATED COLORS

Tones that are closely related, such as yellows and greens, and reds and greens, are "vibrating" colors. The human eye has difficulty distinguishing between the two. This is especially the case for "color blind" Internet users. Avoid use of these vibrating colors to ensure all parts of your ad can be seen clearly.

Google will add a "Feedback - Ad by Google" link near the bottom or corner of the Leaderboard, Banner, and Medium Rectangle sizes. It will be placed at the bottom of Skyscraper ads.

### 2. Apply the Four Color Rule

What is often mistakenly called the "Three Color Rule" is actually a guideline for applying Web colors that should be followed with Image Ads. Specifically, the rule states that one background color (preferably pale) should be used in conjunction with only three foreground colors, hence the "Four Color Rule." A blend of additional foreground colors makes the ad too busy. More than a subtle use of multiple background colors will hamper reading of the foreground colors. The four-color foreground rule of thumb applies to any text that you may incorporate into your Image Ad. The colored text, even if it is black or white, will use up one of your three colors.

### 3. Universal Browser Color Palette

Various Web browsers may display some colors differently than intended. This can wreck havoc with an Image Ad. To be safe, use one of the 216 browser-safe colors. They look the same on every browser for every color monitor. There is not enough space to display them here, but conduct an Internet search on the "216 browser-safe colors" to display them.

## VI.   Ad Units and AdSense

Ad units are grids of AdWord ads shown on Google's Content Network. The most widespread area for ad units is the AdSense program. Ad Units are placed at various spots within AdSense publishers' Websites so that Google can serve tailored ads in these locations on the Content Network. Potential customers benefit since they may learn of discounts or programs in their areas of interest (i.e., the areas that attracted them to the AdSense site in the first place).

When a visitor clicks on one of the ads, Google shares the revenue with the AdSense publisher; i.e., the CPC, just as it does for book publishers with Google Books. The percentage of your CPC Google shares is top secret, but it is thought to be around fifty percent. What does this mean for you as an advertiser? In addition to your ads having the potential to be displayed during the 200 million searches conducted on Google each day, your ads are further displayed on a multitude of other Websites and AdSense sites, including massive retail Websites such as Amazon.com.

### A. Ad Unit Text Boxes

**Leaderboard (728 x 90)**

| Free Telescope Catalog | Celestron Telescope | SkyOptics.com | Telescope Eyepieces |
|---|---|---|---|
| Low prices on dozens of telescopes at Orion's web site. | Minimum prices for Auth. USA Dealer BizRate "Best of the Best" Shop Now | Binoculars, night vision, tripods, rangefinders and telescopes. | A large variety including eyepieces for astrophotography! MaxView |

Ads by Google

**Banner (468 x 60)**

| Free Telescope Catalog | Celestron Telescope |
|---|---|
| Low prices on dozens of telescopes at Orion's web site. | At BizRate's "Excellence" winner for Superb Service & Dealer Prices. |

Ads by Google

## Half Banner (234 x 60)

**Meade, Celestron, & More**
Premier US Meade & Celestron Dealer
25 years of friendly expert service

Ads by Google

## Button (125 x 125)

Ads by Google

**Meade, Celestron, & More**
Premier US Meade & Celestron Dealer 25 years of friendly expert service
www.astronomics.com

## Small Rectangle (180 x 150)

Ads by Google

**Meade, Celestron, & More**
Premier US Meade & Celestron Dealer 25 years of friendly expert service
www.astronomics.com

## Vertical Banner (120 x 240)

Ads by Google

**Meade, Celestron, & More**
Premier US Meade & Celestron Dealer 25 years of friendly expert service
www.astronomics.com

**GPS for Meade Telescopes**
Add GPS to your ETX or LXD55 Scope Fully Integrated Unit - Only $169!
www.scopetronix.com

## Medium Rectangle (300 x 250)

Ads by Google

**SkyOptics.com**
Binoculars, night vision, tripods, rangefinders and telescopes.
www.skyoptics.com

**Celestron Telescope**
Shop for deals on Electronics here! Simply Fast Savings
www.Shopping.com

**Celestron Telescopes**
Shop for deals on Electronics here! Simply Fast Savings
www.Shopping.com

**30-60% Off and Free UPS**
Sale - Telescopes, Spotting Scopes, Binoculars, Accessories, much More
OpticsPlanet.com

## Square (250 x 250)

**Ads by Google**

**Meade, Celestron, & More**
Premier US Meade & Celestron Dealer 25 years of
friendly expert service
www.astronomics.com

**GPS for Meade Telescopes**
Add GPS to your ETX or LXD55 Scope Fully
Integrated Unit - Only $169!
www.scopetronix.com

**ETX Astro accessories**
See our unique range of over 150 accessories to
fit Meade scopes
www.astro-engineering.com

## Large Rectangle (336 x 280)

**Ads by Google**

**Meade, Celestron, & More**
Premier US Meade & Celestron Dealer 25 years of friendly expert
service
www.astronomics.com

**GPS-Mate scope upgrade**
LX200 Classic, Autostar, Gemini No software - just plug & play
www.astro-engineering.com

**GPS for Meade Telescopes**
Add GPS to your ETX or LXD55 Scope Fully Integrated Unit - Only
$169!
www.scopetronix.com

**Free Telescope Catalog**
Special low prices on telescopes at Orion's authoritative website
www.telescope.com

## Skyscraper (120 x 600)

**Ads by Google**

**Free Telescope Catalog**
Low prices on dozens of telescopes at Orion's web site.
www.telescope.com

**Celestron Telescope**
At BizRate's "Excellence" winner for Superb Service & Dealer Prices.
www.BHPhotoVideo.com

**Telescope Eyepieces**
A large variety including eyepieces for astrophotography! MaxView
www.digitalastronomy.cx

**SkyOptics.com**
Binoculars, night vision, tripods, rangefinders and telescopes.
www.skyoptics.com

## Wide Skyscraper (160 x 600)

**Ads by Google**

**Meade, Celestron, & More**
Premier US Meade & Celestron Dealer 25 years of friendly expert service
www.astronomics.com

**GPS for Meade Telescopes**
Add GPS to your ETX or LXD55 Scope Fully Integrated Unit - Only $169!
www.scopetronix.com

**ETX Astro accessories**
See our unique range of over 150 accessories to fit Meade scopes
www.astro-engineering.com

**Shop for Meade Telescope**
Great deals on telescopes. Free bottom-line price comparisons.
www.pricegrabber.com

**Meade telescopes**
Find Sporting Goods at Wal-Mart at Every Day Low Prices!
www.walmart.com

## B. Link Units

Link Units are another form of ad units. They add clickable content to Websites, which allows users to drill down for more information that may not be found within the particular AdSense Website. Here are the various Link Unit sizes.

**5 Links or Less (120 x 90)**

Ads by Google
Orion Telescopes
Meade Telescopes
Goto Telescopes
Vixen Telescopes
Zeiss Telescopes

**4 Links or Less (120 x 90_4)**

Ads by Google
Telescope
Celestron
Binoculars
Meade

**5 Links or Less (160 x 90)**

Ads by Google
Orion Telescopes
Meade Telescopes
Celestron Telescopes
Vixen Telescopes
Galileo Telescopes

**4 Links or Less (160 x 90_4)**

Ads by Google
Binoculars
Bushnell Telescope
Cassegrain
Celestron

**5 Links or Less (180 x 90)**

Ads by Google
Binoculars
Bushnell Refractor Telescope
Canon Telescope
Cassegrain
Celestron

**4 Links or Less (180 x 90_4)**

Ads by Google
Binoculars
Bushnell Telescope
Cassegrain
Celestron

110

**5 Links or Less**
**(200 x 90)**

**4 Links or Less**
**(200 x 90_4)**

Ads by Google
Binoculars
Bushnell Refractor Telescope
Canon Telescope
Cassegrain
Celestron

Ads by Google
Orion Telescopes
Celestron Telescopes
Meade Telescopes UK
Refractor Telescopes

**(458 x 15) – 5 Links or Less**

Ads by Google    Telescopes    Meade ETX    Celestron    Meade LXD75    Meade

**(458 x 15_4) – 4 Links or Less**

Ads by Google    Telescopes    Meade ETX    Celestron    Meade ETX-70AT

**(728 x 15) – 5 Links or Less**

Ads by Google    Meade Telescopes    Refractor Telescopes    Meade ETX    Celestron Telescope    Reflector Telescope

**(728 x 15_4) – 4 Links or Less**

Ads by Google    Meade Telescopes    Celestron Telescopes    Refractor Telescopes    Cassegrain Telescopes

## LINKS OR *LESS*?

Why does Google put the "or less" language in relation to Link Units? Due to its amount of Content Network inventory, Google may not have enough ads to serve up at a particular content site. If this is true, only three titles might be displayed for a "4 Links or Less" Link Unit.

In the past Google only allowed one ad unit to be displayed per page, but now AdSense publishers can run multiple ad units on each page. Below is the maximum number of ad units Google is currently able to support.

| Maximum Ad Units Supported on a Page |
|---|
| ➢ 2 Ad Sense Search Box<br>➢ 1 Link Unit<br>➢ 1 Referral Button<br>➢ 3 Combination of Text or Image Ads |

### C. Themed Ad Units

Just in time for the holidays, Google released themed ad units in 2005. What are they? Themed ad units allow you to display background or watermark drawings behind the words of your text ads. They are only applicable to the Content Network. Here is an example.

## NO CONTROL OVER THE GRAPHICS

> At present, Google does not let you select the graphic that will appear behind the text of your ad.

Themed ads units are a great way to make your ads stand out on the Content Network. If you have one, and you competitor does not, more eyeballs and potential customers will be drawn to your ad. This is a huge advantage for you and a great way to get clicks even if you are not in the top spot.

Google has total control over the drawings displayed on themed ad units and the duration they will show. For example, AdWord advertisers who have this feature enabled will have holiday-themed graphics shown behind the text of their ads from the day after Thanksgiving in the United States until December 26th, the day after Christmas. Google will introduce other graphics for other holidays and special events through out the year, such as the Superbowl. Think of Google as having a giant themed ads switch.

### BE CAREFUL OF HOLIDAY ADS

Once Google disables holiday graphics, this does not mean that your ads enabled with themes will stop showing. You must disable these ads yourself or you will be showing Christmas ads in January.

The graphics are shown in the upper right-hand corner of the ad and may slightly affect the readability of text that is laid over the graphics. Remember, even if you do not have a holiday targeted ad, themed ads are a great way to make it stand out.

### ADSENSE PUBLISHERS CAN DISABLE THEMED AD UNITS

Be mindful that while enabling themes can make your ad stand out, it could also result in less Content sites showing your ads.

### D. GBuy

GBuy is Google's answer to eBay's PayPal. With GBuy, AdWord advertisers can allow secure payments of products and service on their Website. GBuy also lets your customers store their credit card information with Google. As you might expect from Google, this service is free. Google takes a small percentage of the credit card fee. Like themed ad units, having GBuy enabled on your site will make your ads stand out since they will include a GBuy logo next to them in the AdWords column.

### SIGNUP FOR GBUY TODAY

Once Google has fully launched Gbuy, you can sign up for the program at www.gbuy.com

## VII.  Google Foreign Languages and Advertising Regions

### A. Use Foreign Languages to Broaden Your Campaign

Geographic issues can easily arise in your Google marketing campaign given the global reach of the Internet. Fortunately, Google makes it easy to define your advertising by geographic region. You select the language(s) under which your ad will run and then select one of five geographic regions. Google supports over forty different AdWords languages. Each is bolded below. This will give you a quick idea of the countries for which you can target your ads and the particular language in which they can be shown. You can also visit each Google site by using the associated hyperlink. Last, we have also placed an ST next to each language for which Site Targeted ads can be shown.

| Countries | Languages | Google Website |
|---|---|---|
| Albania & Kosovo | Albanian/Tosk | www.google.com/intl/sq/ |
| Andorra | Catalan | www.google.com/intl/ca/ |
| Anguilla | English[ST] | www.google.off.ai/ |
| Antigua and Barbuda | English[ST] | www.google.com.ag/ |
| Argentina | **Spanish**[ST] Guarani | www.google.com.ar/ www.google.com/intl/gn/ |
| Armenia | Armenian Kurdish | www.google.com/intl/hy/ www.google.com/intl/ku/ |
| Austria | German[ST] | www.google.at |
| Australia | English[ST] | www.google.com.au/ |
| Azerbaijan & Georgia & Iran & Turkey | Azeri, **Russian**[ST] Azerbaijani | www.google.az/ www.google.com/intl/az/ |
| Bangladesh | Bengali | www.google.com/intl/bn/ |
| Belarus | Byelorussian | www.google.com/intl/be/ |
| Belgium | **French**[ST]**, Dutch**[ST]**, German**[ST]**, English**[ST] | www.google.be/ |

115

| Belize | English[ST], Spanish[ST] | www.google.com.bz/ |
|---|---|---|
| Bolivia | Spanish[ST] | www.google.com.bo/ |
| Bosnia & Herzegovina | Bosnian, **Serbian**, **Croatian** | www.google.com/intl/bs/ www.google.com/intl/sr/ www.google.com/intl/hr/ |
| Brazil | **Portuguese**[ST] Guarani | www.google.com.br/ www.google.com/intl/gn/ |
| Bulgaria | Bulgarian | www.google.com/intl/bg/ |
| Burundi | French[ST] | www.google.bi/ |
| Canada | French[ST], English[ST] | www.google.ca/ |
| Chad | French[ST] | www.google.td/ |
| Chile | Spanish[ST] | www.google.cl/ |
| China | **Chinese (Simplified)**[ST] **Chinese (Traditional)** Mongolian Uighur | www.google.com/intl/zh-CN/ www.google.com/intl/zh-TW/ www.google.com/intl/mn/ www.google.com/intl/ug/ |
| Colombia | Spanish[ST] | www.google.com.co/ |
| Congo (Republic of) | French[ST] | www.google.cg/ |
| Congo (Democratic Republic of) | French[ST] | www.google.cd/ |
| Cook Islands | English[ST] | www.google.co.ck/ |
| Cocos Islands | English[ST] | www.google.cc/ |
| Costa Rica | **Spanish**[ST] **English**[ST] | www.google.co.cr/ |
| Cote D'Ivoire | French[ST] | www.google.ci/ |
| Croatia | **Croatian** Serbo-Croatian | www.google.com/intl/hr/ www.google.com/intl/sh/ |
| Cuba | Spanish[ST] | www.google.com.cu/ |
| Czech Republic | Czech | www.google.com/intl/cs/ |
| Denmark | **Danish**[ST], Faroese | www.google.dk/ www.google.com/intl/da/ |
| Djibouti | French[ST], Arabic | www.google.dj/ |
| Dominican Republic | Spanish[ST] | www.google.com.do/ |
| Dubai, Egypt, Iraq, Jordan, Kuwait, Lebanon, Oman, Sudan, Saudi Arabia, Syria, UAE | Arabic | www.google.com/intl/ar/ www.google.com.sa/ |

| | | |
|---|---|---|
| Ecuador | Spanish[ST] | www.google.com.ec/ |
| El Salvador | Spanish[ST] | www.google.com.sv/ |
| English-Speaking Countries | Pig Latin | www.google.com/intl/xx-piglatin/ |
| Eritrea & Ethiopia (North) | Tigrinya | www.google.com/intl/ti/ |
| Estonia | Estonian | www.google.com/intl/et/ |
| Ethiopia (south) | Amharic | www.google.com/intl/am/ |
| Faroe Islands | Faroese, **Danish**[ST] | www.google.com/intl/fo/<br>www.google.com/intl/da/ |
| Fiji Islands | English[ST] | www.google.com.fj/ |
| France<br>-Bretagne<br>-Languedoc Roussillon, Midi-Pyrénées<br>-Basque | **French**[ST], Berrichon<br>-Breton<br>-Occitan<br>-Catalan<br>-Basque | www.google.fr/<br>www.google.com/intl/br/<br>www.google.com/intl/oc/<br>www.google.com/intl/ca/<br>www.google.com/intl/eu/ |
| Finland | **Finnish**[ST]<br>**Swedish**[ST] | www.google.fi/<br>www.google.com/intl/sv/ |
| Gambia | English[ST] | www.google.gm/ |
| Georgia & Azerbaijan & Iran & Turkey | Georgian | www.google.com/intl/ka/ |
| Germany<br>-Schleswig-Holstein | **German**[ST]<br>-Frisian | www.google.de/<br>www.google.com/intl/fy/ |
| Ghana | Twi | www.google.com/intl/tw/ |
| Gibraltar | **English**[ST], **Spanish**[ST], **Italian**[ST], **Portuguese**[ST] | www.google.com.gi/ |
| Greece | Greek | www.google.com/intl/el/<br>www.google.com.gr/ |
| Greenland | English[ST], Danish[ST] | www.google.gl/ |
| Guatemala | Spanish[ST] | www.google.com.gt/ |
| Guam, Saïpan, Oceania | Chamorro | www.google.com/intl/gu/ |
| Guernsey | French[ST], English[ST] | www.google.co.gg/ |
| Honduras | Spanish[ST] | www.google.hn/ |
| Hong Kong | **Chinese (Traditional)** | www.google.com.hk/ |
| Hungary | Hungarian[ST] | www.google.co.hu/<br>www.google.com/intl/hu/ |
| Korea | Korean[ST] | www.google.co.kr/ |

| Country | Language | URL |
|---|---|---|
| India | **English**[ST] | www.google.co.in/ |
| | **Hindi** | www.google.com/intl/hi/ |
| | Kannada | www.google.com/intl/kn/ |
| | Marathi | www.google.com/intl/mr/ |
| | Oriya | www.google.com/intl/or/ |
| | Punjabi | www.google.com/intl/pa/ |
| | Tamil | www.google.com/intl/ta/ |
| | Telegu | www.google.com/intl/te/ |
| | **Urdu** | www.google.com/intl/ur/ |
| | Bengali (Bengla) | www.google.com/intl/bn/ |
| | Bihari | www.google.com/intl/ml/ |
| | Malayalam | www.google.com/intl/ug/ |
| | Uighur | www.google.com/intl/sd/ |
| | Sindhi | |
| Indonesia | **Indonesian** | www.google.co.id/ |
| | Bahasa, **Indonesian** | www.google.com/intl/id/ |
| | Sundanese | www.google.com/intl/su/ |
| Indonesia-Jawi Island | Javanese | www.google.com/intl/jw/ |
| Iran & Iraq & UAE | Perse (Farsi) | www.google.com/intl/fa/ |
| | Kurdish | www.google.com/intl/ku/ |
| Ireland | **English**[ST] | www.google.ie |
| | Gaelic Irish | www.google.com/intl/ga/ |
| Iceland | Icelandic | www.google.com/intl/is/ |
| Israel | **Hebrew** | www.google.co.il/ |
| | **Arabic** | www.google.com/intl/ar/ |
| | Yiddish | www.google.com/intl/yi/ |
| Italy<br>-Piemonte, Liguria, Calabria<br>-Sardinia | **Italian**[ST]<br>• Occitan<br>• Catalan | www.google.it/<br>www.google.com/intl/oc/<br>www.google.com/intl/ca/ |
| Jamaica | English[ST] | www.google.com.jm/ |
| Japan | Japanese[ST] | www.google.co.jp/ |
| Jersey Island | French[ST], English[ST] | www.google.co.je/ |
| Kazakhstan | Kazakh | www.google.kz/ |
| | Uighur | www.google.com/intl/ug/ |
| Kenya | **English**[ST] | www.google.co.ke/ |
| | Kiswahili | www.google.com/intl/sw/ |
| Kyrgyzstan | Kyrgyz | www.google.kg/ |
| | Uighur | www.google.com/intl/ky/ |
| | | www.google.com/intl/ug/ |

| | | |
|---|---|---|
| Laos | Laothian | www.google.com/intl/lo/ |
| Latvia | Latvian | www.google.lv/ |
| Lesotho | **English**[ST], Zulu<br>Sesotho | www.google.co.ls/<br>www.google.com/intl/st/ |
| Libya | Arabic, Italian[ST], English[ST] | www.google.com.ly/ |
| Liechtenstein | German[ST] | www.google.li/ |
| Lithuania | Lithuanian | www.google.lt/ |
| Luxembourg | German[ST] | www.google.lu/ |
| Macedonia | Macedonian, **Serbian**,<br>**Croatian** | www.google.com/intl/mk/<br>www.google.com/intl/sr/<br>www.google.com/intl/hr/ |
| Malaysia | Bahasa Melayu, **English**[ST]<br>Bahasa Melayu<br>Tamil<br>Malayalam | www.google.com.my/<br>www.google.com/intl/ms/<br>www.google.com/intl/ta/<br>www.google.com/intl/ml/ |
| Malawi | English[ST] | www.google.mw/ |
| Malta | Maltese | www.google.com/intl/mt/<br>www.google.com.mt/ |
| Mauritius | French[ST], English[ST] | www.google.mu/ |
| Mexico | Spanish[ST] | www.google.com.mx/ |
| Micronesia | English[ST] | www.google.fm/ |
| Mongolia | Mongolian | www.google.com/intl/mn/<br>www.google.mn/ |
| Montserrat | English[ST] | www.google.ms/ |
| Mozambique | Zulu, **Portuguese**[ST] | www.google.com/intl/pt/<br>www.google.com/intl/zu/ |
| Namibia | **English**[ST], Afrikaans | www.google.com.na/ |
| Nepal | Nepali | www.google.com/intl/ne/<br>www.google.com.np/ |
| Netherlands<br>-Friesland | **Dutch**[ST]<br>-Frisian | www.google.nl/<br>www.google.com/intl/fy/ |
| New Zealand | English[ST] | www.google.co.nz/ |
| Nicaragua | Spanish[ST] | www.google.com.ni/ |
| Norfolk | English[ST] | www.google.com.nf/ |
| Norway | Norwegian[ST]<br>Norwegian (Bokmål)<br>Norwegian (Nynorsk) | www.google.no/<br>www.google.com/intl/no/<br>www.google.com/intl/nn/ |

| | | |
|---|---|---|
| Pakistan | Punjabi<br>Sindhi<br>Uighur | www.google.com.pk/<br>www.google.com/intl/sd/<br>www.google.com/intl/ug/ |
| Panama | Spanish[ST], English[ST] | www.google.com.pa/ |
| Paraguay | **Spanish**[ST]<br>Guarani | www.google.com.py/<br>www.google.com/intl/gn/ |
| Peru | Spanish[ST] | www.google.com.pe/ |
| Philippines | Filipino **Tagalog** | www.google.com.ph/<br>www.google.com/intl/tl/ |
| Pitcairn (Islands) | English[ST] | www.google.pn/ |
| Poland & Lituania | Polish[ST] | www.google.pl/ |
| Portugal & Angola & Brazil & Mozambique | Portuguese[ST] | www.google.com/intl/pt/ |
| Puerto Rico | Spanish[ST] | www.google.com.pr/ |
| Roman Empire | Latina | www.google.com/intl/la/ |
| Romania & Moldova | **Romanian, German**[ST], **Hungarian**[ST] | www.google.ro/<br>www.google.com/intl/ro/ |
| Russia | Russian[ST] | www.google.com.ru/<br>www.google.com/intl/ru/ |
| Rwanda | **French**[ST], Swahili, **English**[ST] | www.google.rw/ |
| Saint Helena | English[ST] | www.google.sh/ |
| Saint Vincent and the Grenadines | English[ST] | www.google.com.vc/ |
| Samoa | English[ST] | www.google.as/ |
| San-Marino | Italian[ST] | www.google.sm/ |
| Scotland | **English**[ST], Scots Gaelic | www.google.com/intl/gd/ |
| Seychelles | **French**[ST], **English**[ST] | www.google.sc/ |
| Serbia | **Serbian**<br>Serbo-Croatian | www.google.com/intl/sr/<br>www.google.com/intl/sh/ |
| Singapore | Tamoul<br>Malay Bahasa | www.google.com.sg/<br>www.google.com/intl/ta/<br>www.google.com/intl/ms/ |
| Slovakia | Slovak, Hungarian[ST] | www.google.sk/<br>www.google.com/intl/sk/ |

| | | |
|---|---|---|
| Slovenia | Slovenian | www.google.com/intl/sl/ |
| Somalia | Somalia | www.google.com/intl/so/ |
| South Africa | English[ST]<br>Afrikaans<br>Xhosa<br>Zulu<br>Sesotho | www.google.co.za/<br>www.google.com/intl/af/<br>www.google.com/intl/xh/<br>www.google.com/intl/zu/<br>www.google.com/intl/st/ |
| Spain<br>-Basque Country<br>-Cataluna<br>-Galicia<br>-Val D'Aran | **Spanish**[ST], Basque, **Catalan**,<br>Galician,<br>• Basque<br>• Catalan<br>• Galician<br>• Occitan | www.google.es/<br>www.google.com/intl/es/<br>www.google.com/intl/eu/<br>www.google.com/intl/ca/<br>www.google.com/intl/gl/<br>www.google.com/intl/oc/ |
| Sweden | Swedish[ST] | www.google.se/<br>www.google.com/intl/sv/ |
| Sri Lanka | Tamil<br>Sinhalese | www.google.com/intl/ta/<br>www.google.com/intl/si/ |
| Switzerland | **German**[ST], **Italian**[ST]<br>Romanche | www.google.ch/<br>www.google.com/intl/rm/ |
| Taiwan | **Chinese (Traditional)** | www.google.com.tw/ |
| Tajikistan | **English**[ST], Tajik | www.google.com.tj/ |
| Tanzania | Kiswahili | www.google.com/intl/sw/ |
| Thailand, Vietnam | Thai | www.google.com/intl/th/<br>www.google.co.th/ |
| Tonga | English[ST] | www.google.to/ |
| Trinidad and Tobago | **English**[ST], **French**[ST],<br>**Spanish**[ST], **Chinese<br>(Traditional), Chinese<br>(Simplified)**[ST] | www.google.tt/ |
| Turkey | **Turkish**[ST]<br>Kurdish<br>Uighur | www.google.com/intl/tr/<br>www.google.com.tr/<br>www.google.com/intl/ku/<br>www.google.com/intl/ug/ |
| Turkmenistan | Turkmen | www.google.com/intl/tk/<br>www.google.tm/ |
| Uganda | English[ST] | www.google.co.ug/ |
| Ukraine | Ukrainian | www.google.com/intl/uk/<br>www.google.com.ua/ |
| United Arab Emirates | Arabic | www.google.ae/ |

| United States of America | **English**[ST] **Spanish** | www.google.com/ www.google.com/intl/es/ |
|---|---|---|
| Uruguay | Spanish[ST] | www.google.com.uy/ |
| Uzbekistan & Afghanistan & Kazakhstan & Tajikistan & Turkmenistan | Uzbek Uighur | www.google.com/intl/uz/ www.google.uz/ www.google.com/intl/ug/ |
| United Kingdom | **English**[ST] Scots Gaelic Gaelic Irish Welsh | www.google.co.uk/ www.google.com/intl/gd/ www.google.com/intl/ga/ www.google.com/intl/cy/ |
| Ukraine | Ukrainian | www.google.com/intl/uk/ www.google.com.ua/ |
| Vietnam & Cambodia & Laos | **Vietnamese, French**[ST]**, Chinese (Traditional)** | www.google.com.vn/ www.google.com/intl/vi/ |
| Virgin Islands | English[ST] | www.google.vg/ www.google.co.vi/ |
| Wales | Welsh | www.google.com/intl/cy/ |
| World | Interlingua Esperanto | www.google.com/intl/ia/ www.google.com/intl/eo/ |
| Yugoslavia | **Serbian**, Montenegrin, Albanian, **Hungarian**[ST], **Slovak, Romanian**, Serbo-Croatian | www.google.com/intl/sr/ www.google.com/intl/sq/ www.google.com/intl/hu/ www.google.com/intl/sk/ www.google.com/intl/ro/ www.google.com/intl/sh/ |

## HOW TO TRACK PERFORMANCE BY COUNTRY

Google does not enable you to track clicks by country/region within the same campaign. To remedy this, set up campaigns by country/region and then you will be tacking clicks from that country/region only.

If you are a seller on the Internet, you may have an international marketplace into which you sell products or at least different geographic regions. Be mindful of alternate terms for your products in these markets. Soft drinks are called "soda" in much of the Southern United States, "pop" in the Midwest, and "soft drinks" in most regions around the country.

---

### Keywords in Different Languages

Keywords in many languages are reversed from the English version. Take, for instance, Spanish.

English user search:          **"Cilantro Chilies Verde"**
Spanish user search:          **"Chilies Verde Cilantro"**

Thankfully with AdWord ads *any* keyword is bolded no matter what order it is displayed.

Another example is soccer. In Mexico, and most other countries, soccer is called "football." For the U.S. market simply have a listing for the keyword "soccer" instead of "football."

United States user search:          **"Soccer"**
Other country user search:          **"Football"**

Google allows you to target English-speaking countries, just keep in mind that while many Spanish Americans use English keyboards, they type words in Spanish, but Google will flag them as English being from the US.

---

## USE GOOGLE'S FREE LANGUAGE TRANSLATIONS

> One of the Internet's best free language translation sites is offered by none other than Google. Visit http://Google.com/ and click on the link next to the search box called "Language Tools" to translate your keywords into the various languages of your target market.

If you speak a language other than the standard English language in which AdWords homepage is set, you can easily change your language preferences under the "User Preferences" section of the "My Account" tab.

### B. Use Geographic Regions to Your Advantage

When creating a new campaign, you will be presented with five geographic regions from which you may choose.

**Target customers by location**

How large is the area where you'd like your ad to appear? Choose one:

- ⦿ **Countries and territories** - Your ads will appear for searches made anywhere in the locations you select.

- ○ **Regions and cities** - Your ads will appear for searches made in the regions and cities you choose. (Not available in all locations.)

- ○ **Customized** - Your ads will appear for searches made within a specific distance from your business or other location you choose.

[ Continue » ]

How does Google know if a person is searching in a particular region? There are two ways. The first is when the searcher uses a city or state name in the search itself.

Google
Web · Images · Groups · News · Froogle · Local^New! · more »

Memphis Barbeque Sauce

Advanced Search
Preferences
Language Tools

[ Google Search ] [ I'm Feeling Lucky ]

Google may also compare the Internet Protocol (IP) address with a database to determine where the searcher is located. If the searcher's Internet Service Provider (ISP) uses a proxy server, Google will be unable to determine the IP address of the searcher. If Google cannot determine either, it will default to global/nationwide ads.

**Five Google Geographic Regions**

1. Global
2. Nationwide
3. Regions
4. Cities
5. Custom

### 1. Global Region

The global region is self-explanatory. It spans all 240 countries under the Google umbrella. If this is your target market and you are selling physical products, you truly must have a product that can be shipped virtually anywhere. This will likely require the consultation of a law firm dealing in international trade to ensure international trademark, copyright and patent laws will not be violated, designation of origin, import/export laws of the various countries, etc.

### REMEMBER TIME ZONE DIFFERENCES

For North American advertisers, the early morning may be the highest traffic time for customers in Europe. Google is tied to Pacific Standard Time, which means the Google advertising day beings at 8 GST. For European advertisers, Americans will not be viewing your ads until late in the Google day.

Unlike traditional advertising, Google charges you the same amount per click (from the amount you set) if you are advertising locally to a very small market or globally to millions of people. If your products or services reach a global or national region, your ad will be seen more often and you will be paying the same CPC as if you were advertising to a local market of a thousand people. It's also a free way to build brand recognition in a country or internationally.

### 2. National Region

The nationwide region is also self-explanatory. This region spans any of the 240 countries under the Google umbrella. This will be the target market for most companies selling physical products that have a national reach such as appliances, automobile parts, books, hair care products, and others. This is an undesirable region if you are offering local services such as restaurants, house cleaning services, lawn services, etc.

### 3. Amazon-Specific Marketing Campaign

Amazon.com seeks to be the Internet's largest retailer. Under its Advantage and Marketplace Programs, sellers of products can list items on Amazon.com and reach its millions of users. Imagine coupling this reach with your Google advertising campaign. If your products are offered through Amazon, you can set up Google ads that target the six country regions in which Amazon has established stores. Apart from the United States, Amazon has international Websites targeting Austria, Canada, United Kingdom, Germany, France, and Japan. Each ad impression will have a link to a different Web page within your overall Website. For example, one of your ads may be in French and only appear to Google users in France. Your URL will link to a French page within your Website that, in turn, links to www.Amazon.fr (Amazon's French Website). A more direct approach would be to link directly to www.Amazon.fr from your Google ad. To do this, however, the ad must show that you are an affiliate as discussed below.

## KNOW YOUR DISTRIBUTOR

Ensure that the distributor for your product, ships to the country/region in which you are targeting.

## 4. States and Metropolitan Regions

The key to the states and metropolitan regions of Google is first determining how they are defined. Google gives you the option of choosing between entire states within a country or major metropolitan areas. For example, San Francisco-San Jose-Oakland is a metropolitan area in the State of California that you will have the option to select.

## METROPOLITAN REGIONS MAY REACH MULTIPLE STATES

Metropolitan regions may span state borders. For example, Rochester, Minnesota-Mason City, Iowa is a region that you will have the option of selecting within Google.

All regions within Google's 240 countries are not available under the states and metropolitan option. This will be the target market for most companies selling physical products that have a regional appeal such as restaurant or food stores selling items of regional flavor, sports companies selling memorabilia for certain college and professional teams, and others. This is also a desirable option if you are offering metropolitan/region services such as tickets to concerts, the theatre, sporting events, etc. These are great markets if you want to start out small with your business and focus on a limited target market before branching out.

## BE CAREFUL WHERE YOU ARE SHIPPING

> Check with your attorney on shipments of certain products into various regions around the world. Wine, for example, is precluded from being shipped into certain U.S. states.

## 5. Google Local and Cities Region

Google Local crosschecks Yellow Page information with data culled from over 8 billion Web pages to offer search results focused on neighborhood businesses.

### a. Use of Google Local

Use of Google Local is easy; a searcher merely inputs a zip code or a town/city name along with a search term at http://local.google.com and the following is displayed.

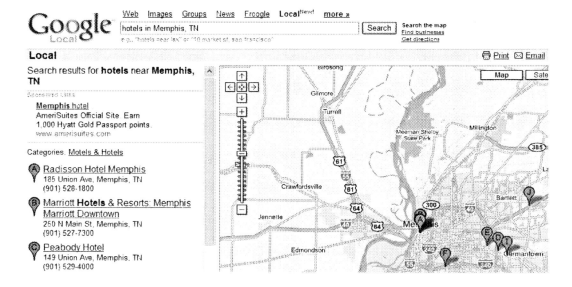

A Google map showing locations of the various businesses you are searching on is shown. You can then zoom in on the map view or select the satellite or hybrid views to locate your business.

## ADWORDS ADS WITHIN GOOGLE LOCAL SEARCH RESULTS

> Google shows an impression of the top ranking AdWords text ad above the search results in Google Local. The second and third ranking ads are shown at the bottom of the page below the search results.

What is the "Remember this location" check box under the Google Local search? It is simply a way for Google, by depositing a cookie on your computer, to automatically remember your local area of search for future reference so that you do not have to key in the zip code or location each time.

## LIMITED TARGET CITIES

> Google does not offer target markets in *every* city of the 240 countries; only major cities outside the United States.

Here's all you have to do to get your business listed free with Google Local:

### Add Your Business on Google Local Today

1. Email an inquiry to: Local-Listings@Google.com
2. Google will respond and ask for details about your business.
3. Upon response your business will be included in Google Local.

### b. Transit Trip Planner

Google has recently been testing a tool called the Transit Trip Planner, which gives commuters public transportation schedules and information before they begin their journey. The same map and tools used for Google Local apply here. Pricing data for the cost of the trip is given for all transit methods including by vehicle (IRS standard cost per mile data is used) to let commuters know which method is best.

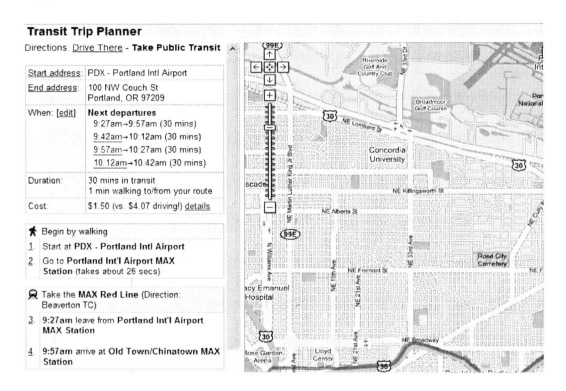

AdWord ads are currently not displayed in Google's Transit Trip Planner, but look for this to change in the future. Also, watch for the functionality and usability of Google's Transit Trip Planner to increase in the future.

### 6. Custom Region

If you do not want a circular area to define the meets and bounds of your local market, Google allows you to define the market by creating any shape using latitude and longitude points (e.g., 35* 20' 31", -120* 5' 42"). The asterisk signifies degrees. This may appear like you'll need to take a navigation class to learn how to do this, but Google once again makes it simple. The following Websites will display latitude and longitude coordinates that you can plug into Google: Maporama.com, Maptools.com and Multimap.com.

In the Custom Region at least three latitude and longitude points are required to set the boundaries on your target geographical area. This will create a triangle. If you want to cover a different shaped area such as a rectangle, a fourth point will have to be added. The most common Google custom region is a circle drawn on Google Maps. Google recommends a circle that is at least twenty miles or thirty-five kilometers in diameter.

Other custom marketing areas that are separate will require a new AdWords campaign to be created. This may sound expensive, but don't worry. Unlike traditional advertising programs, there is no extra charge from Google for the number of campaigns you set up. You are only limited by your creativity and daily amount that you wish to spend.

### TRACKING CLICK-THROUGH RATES

Google returns different click-through results for each country and language. This may sound difficult to track, but Google does all the tracking for you.

Because Google Maps is now an integrated part of AdWords, you can use it to define your Custom Region. In the Custom Region, Google lets you define a set region from the location of your business or a very specific target market. In this instance you'll have to enter your business address. This target market is defined by a set distance (miles, yards, etc) from your place of business. Think of creating a circle that defines a marketing area around your business or target market. The distance you provide Google is the radius of the circle.

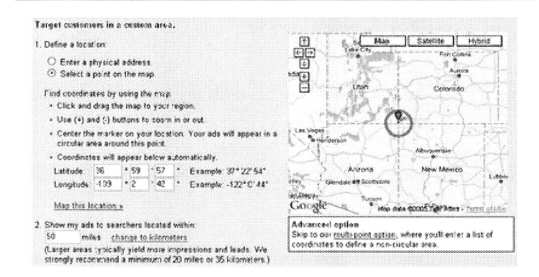

To set your custom location with just a few mouse clicks, select custom targeting when starting a new campaign. Select the map (Coordinate Tool) and zoom in on your target location. By changing the distance you will change the diameter of the customer circle area.

## AREA LIMITATIONS

While you will be able to define almost any size area on Google Maps, the AdWords system has its limitations. It is not able to target an area as specific as a city block.

## VIII. AdWords Optimization Tools

Google offers a number of free tools that are very powerful in optimizing your AdWords marketing campaign. We will discuss each in detail below.

---

**Four AdWords Management Tools**

➢ Keyword Tool
➢ Traffic Estimator Tool
➢ Negative Keywords Tool
➢ Site Exclusion Tool

---

### A. Keyword Tool

To help focus your advertising campaign, Google has a tool to more narrowly define your broad search terms. Google provides—free of charge—a powerful Keyword Tool to optimize ads for your target market.

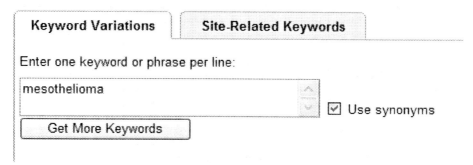

When you input your broad search term it returns more specific search terms users have used including your broad search term. You can search for similar keywords, search volume on those keywords, and the average CPC advertisers are paying. You can also get detailed results for each of Google's 240 countries and various foreign languages.

## FINDING KEYWORDS IN YOUR ACCOUNT IS EASY

If you have a large advertising campaign, it is hard to keep track of how each keyword is performing. To search for a keyword in your account, all you must do is type it into the search box located in the upper right corner on your Campaign Management pages.

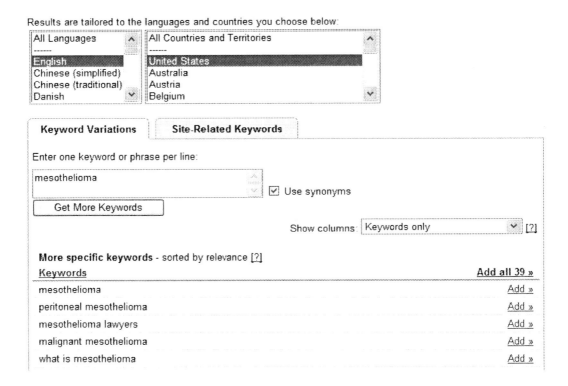

For each keyword you create, the Keyword Tool will return search terms culled from the 20 million searches conducted daily on Google that are variations of your keyword or associated in common searches. This is one of the best tools Google offers and its inner workings will be key to your marketing success. When compiling your ad you'll be asked to input all keywords for which you would like your ad to appear when Google users search on those terms.

Then, Google provides a tool that displays search terms users employ similar to your own. This includes common misspellings and alternative queries if you check the synonyms box. Consider:

| Keyword | Possible Keyword Tool Results |
|---|---|
| Rice | Basmati Rice<br>Brown Rice<br>Growing Rice<br>Long Grain Rice<br>Long-Grain Rice<br>Longrain Rice<br>Rice-a-Roni<br>Rice Recipes<br>Spanish Rice<br>Sticky Rice<br>Sushi Rice<br>White Rice<br>Wild Rice |

## SEE THE MINIMUM BIDS FOR YOUR KEYWORDS

You can view minimum bids for your keywords by either viewing them in the Ad Group details page or by running a custom report.

Within the Keyword Tool you can also generate keywords based upon the text used in a particular Website. Run your landing page through this generator and see what keywords come out the other end.

Results are tailored to **English, United States** Edit

| Keyword Variations | Site-Related Keywords |
|---|---|

Enter a webpage URL to find keywords related to the content on the page. [?]

[                                          ]  Get keywords

*Example: www.example.com/catalog/product?id=71828*

☐ Include other pages on my site linked from this URL

## CHECK OUT COMPETITOR'S WEBSITES

> You can also run competitor's Websites through this tool to learn what keywords they may be focusing on that you are missing!

### B. Traffic Estimator Tool

Google's free Traffic Estimator Tool allows you to get traffic estimates for up to 5000 keywords *before* adding them to your account.

**Traffic Estimator Options**

1. Select keywords (keyword=Broad Match; "keyword"=Phrase Match; [keyword]=Exact Match; -keyword=Negative Match);
2. Maximum Cost-Per-Click (CPC) or let Google do it for you, which will return a value with a #1 rank 85% of the time;
3. Select a target language;
4. Select the region (Global/National, Regions and Cities, or Customized); and
5. Select from the list of countries or simply select "All Countries."

**Traffic Estimator**

Get quick traffic estimates for new keywords without adding them to an account or using the AdWords sign-up wizard.

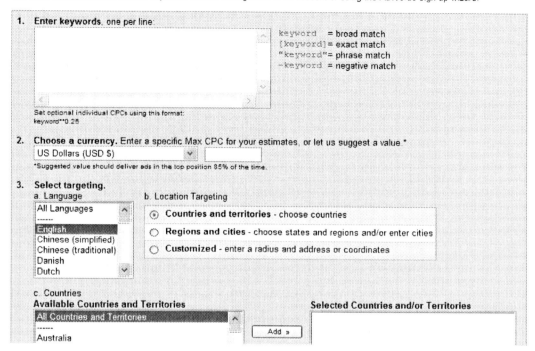

This powerful tool will give you an estimated ad position in the AdWords column per keyword based on your maximum CPC and the CTR the keywords are already getting on Google. You also receive estimated clicks per day and cost per day and the average you will pay on a CPC basis.

**Traffic Estimator**

« Revise settings | Download as .csv

Max CPC: USD $0.10
Recommended daily budget: USD $3.00

| Keywords | Avg. Position | Clicks / Day | Cost / Day | Avg. CPC |
|----------|---------------|--------------|------------|----------|
| Overall | 8.5 | 17.0 | $1.45 | $0.09 |

Before you spend any money on Google, its Traffic Estimator Tool will provide the rating it forecasts for your ad on all keywords you've selected. Adjust your ad *before* you are spending advertising dollars to maximize your ROI.

## PLACEMENT FOR BEST RECOGNITION

If a user has their browser set in "normal view," the number of ads shown in the AdWords column is reduced to only five without scrolling plus two in the "blue." If bidding for the top position is too expensive, reduce the top position CPC amount in the Traffic Estimator to meet your CPC budget and ensure the average position is still 1-7. This is an *average* position estimate. Even the 4th average position may appear in the 2nd spot at times and the 6th at others.

### Use the Big Three in Competitive Data Gathering

1. Competitors within the top positions – Follow URL links within AdWords search results column;
2. Keywords competitors are bidding on – Use Keyword Estimator Tool as shown above and AdWords search results column; and
3. How much competitors are paying for keywords – Use combinations of Keyword Estimator and Keyword Tools as shown above.

## ALTERNATE TRAFFIC ESTIMATOR TOOL

Another powerful and free tool that combines both a keyword and traffic estimator can be found at www.123Promotion.co.uk. This free tool not only gives daily and monthly forecasts, but also forecasts how many clicks a keyword is likely to be receiving five years down the road. This is a great way to see if you have a product that is in a declining market as well as a great traffic estimator for the immediate future.

## C. Negative Keyword Tool

Use Google's Negative Keyword Tool to select negative keywords or simply place a minus sign in front of a word when entering it in the Keyword or Traffic Estimator Tools. If your negative keyword is "New Jersey," anyone searching on "New Jersey Lemon Laws" will not see an impression of your ad. You can use Google's Clean Sweep algorithm to easily replace negative keywords at the Ad Group level and replace them at the Campaign level.

**Edit Campaign Negative Keywords**

Campaign: Campaign #2 ▾ [Go]

Negative keywords prevent your ads from appearing for queries containing the word [?] The negative keywords you select here will apply to all Ad Groups within this campaign.

**Add new campaign negative keywords**                    Need ideas? Keyword Tool

**Enter words manually...**

**... or use Clean Sweep.**
Do your negative keywords appear in more than one Ad Group? Remove them from the Ad Group level, and add them at the campaign level.

1. Find negative keywords occurring in  all Ad Groups ▾

2. Delete from Ad Groups and add as campaign negative keywords.
You'll have the chance to confirm each change.

[ Add Keywords ]                    [ Run Clean Sweep ]

## GOOGLE SEARCH YOUR KEYWORDS

Conduct a search on "Florida Lemon Laws." If terms relating to Florida lemon growing ordinances appear, add these as negative keywords. Scan over a couple pages of the search results to ensure you get a good selection of negative keywords.

## D. Site Exclusion Tool

Google's powerful Site Exclusion Tool allows you to block your ads from showing on up to 500 Content Network Websites. This is the Negative Keywords Tool for domains instead of keywords.

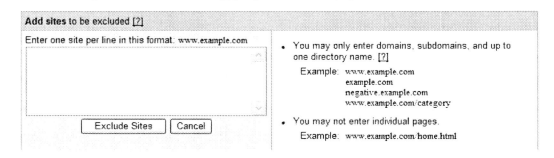

Keep in mind that excluding a site will exclude your ad from showing on *all* pages of that Website. The Site Exclusion is very powerful, but it can work against you.

## REMEMBER SITE SECTIONS

If there are a few pages that will gain you customers, use Site Sections to target only those particular pages on which your ad will be displayed.

### E. AdWords Editor

Google's AdWords Editor is a program that you download to your hard drive so that you can make changes without being on the Internet. This is a huge benefit you travel often and need to update your account on the fly.

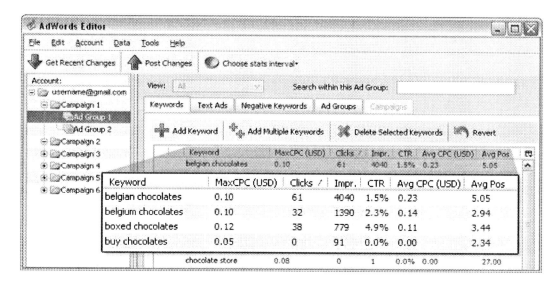

You can do everything you can online with the AdWords Editor except use Google's tools, such as the Keyword Tool, to get the most relevant search data. With the AdWords Editor you can make bulk ad or keyword changes, search within your account, generate reports, view statistics and check for account errors.

### DOWNLOAD THE ADWORDS EDITOR TODAY

To download this powerful advertising tool, please visit www.adwordseditor.google.com

### IX. Content Network Targeting and Bid Strategies

#### A. Content Network Targeting

We have explained in detail Google's Content Network that reaches some of the most visited sites on the Internet including AdSense sites and *The New York Times*. On the Content Network information usually takes the form of lengthy articles on various topics. Obviously some will attract the very kind of Internet users that will be interested in your products. Others, well, let's just say you couldn't buy clicks from these readers for your products or services. Now you no longer have to wait for Internet searchers to look for your keywords. You can now show your ads where content is right there waiting for you on sites that receive the eyes of a known demographic of users. Google has developed two new options for your AdWords campaign on the Content Network along with a powerful tool to implement them.

#### 1. Site Targeting

The first option is called Site Targeting and it changes the rules for traditional Google advertising. With Site Targeting, you pick the particular *Website(s)* on the Content Network where you want your ads to run. With the traditional way you pick the *keywords* that will run across the entire network and then trigger your ads. This is AdWords inside out. Here you pay under a Cost-Per-Impression ("CPM") model that is based on 1000 impressions of your ad. The sites that typically work the best are small, content-rich Blogs and Websites that target your particular audience.

#### PAY THE SAME REGARDLESS OF CLICKS

With Site Targeting, you pay the same amount for advertising on key Content Network sites no matter how many clicks you get!

## a. CPM Costs

Okay. Fine. What is this going to cost you? There is good news. Google has dropped the minimum CPM to only $0.25 USD. You can now get 1000 impressions of your ad on key Content Network sites for only $0.25. If your Click-Through-Rate is at the normal 1.0% level, this means you will get 10 clicks for $.25, which equals $0.025 per click! If your CTR is around 5%, you will get 50 clicks per 1000 and have the potential of paying only $0.005 per click (i.e., less than a penny per click).

| Minimum CPM | Maximum CPM |
|---|---|
| $0.25 USD | Unlimited |

It is important to realize that Site Targeted ads compete for placement with normal keyword targeted ads. This means you still must bid your CPM competitively on popular Content Network sites to get top placement.

### CERTAIN ADSENSE SITES MAY HAVE A LOW CTR

Some AdSense sites that you target may only yield a 0.1% CTR and this will skew your normal ROI. The great thing is that you can easily monitor poorly performing Content Network sites and delete those where your ad is not receiving clicks. This is called Google's Site Exclusion Tool and we will discuss it below.

If you do not have a particular site in mind, but would like to find out which sites relating to your keywords are showing Google ads, you can simply enter your keywords into Google's Site Tool and it will return a list of Websites relevant to those keywords. Here are the steps.

### b. Site Target Setup

There are three quick steps to setting up a Site Targeted Campaign instead of a keywords targeted Campaign.

---

## How to Set Up a Site Targeted Campaign

➤ First, create a new Campaign and select the "Site Targeted Campaign" option.

➤ Second, pick the languages and regions you want to target.

➤ Third, create your Site Target ad and list your keywords. Google will then return a list of sites that are running AdSense ads and have content with your designated keywords.

---

| Campaign Management | Reports | Analytics | My Account |
|---|---|---|---|

Campaign Summary | Tools | Conversion Tracking

**New Site-targeted Campaign Setup**

Target customers > Create ad > Target ad > Set pricing > Set daily budget > Review and save

**Target ad: choose sites**

Use the Site Tool below to pick the sites where your ads may appear.  Tell me how to use this tool.

| ☐ Available sites | Max. Impressions/Day  [?] | | Selected sites |
|---|---|---|---|
| ☐ expressfind.com | 0k-1 | | |
| ☐ sunengine.com | 0k-1 | | |
| ☐ surffast.com | 0k-1 | Add » | |
| ☐ newssearch.looksmart.com | 0k-1 | « Remove | |
| ☐ incywincy.com | 0k-1 | | |

## Site Targeted Campaign Set Up Continued

> ➤ You can then select from the list or manually type in the sites you want to target. Next Google will ask you for the amount you are willing to pay per 1000 impressions of your ads on these sites.

| Campaign Management | Reports | Analytics | My Account |
|---|---|---|---|

Campaign Summary | Tools | Conversion Tracking

### New Site-targeted Campaign Setup

Target customers  >  Create ad  >  Target ad  >  **Set pricing**  >  Set daily budget  >  Review and save

| selected sites | Max Impressions / Day: |
|---|---|
| 2 Sites that allow image or text ads | 10k-100k |
| 0 Sites that allow text ads only | 0k-10k |
| **Total — All selected sites** | **10k-100k** |
| These represent the impressions available to all advertisers, NOT your total impressions. We recommend that you set an affordable bid, run your ads for a few days, then adjust your sites and max CPM accordingly. | |

### Set pricing: Cost per thousand impressions (CPM)

The maximum CPM [?] is the top amount you're willing to pay each 1000 times your ad is displayed. The the better the chance that your ad will show. Your CPM must be at least $0.25.

Maximum CPM for sites in this Ad Group: $ 0.25

## Site Targeted Campaign Set Up Continued

> ➤ Finally, you set your daily budget, review your selections, and your ads begin showing.

Google also allows you to *exclude* sites where you do not want impressions of your ads being shown.

## EXCLUDE UP TO 500 SITES

Google's powerful Site Exclusion Tool allows you to block your ads from showing on up to 500 Websites. This is like the Negative Keywords Tool on steroids. Keep in mind that excluding a site will exclude your ad from showing on *all* pages of that Website. If there are a few pages that will gain you customers, use Site Sections (discussed below) to target only those particular pages on which your ad will be displayed.

### c. Site Targeted Languages

Google supports eighteen Site Target languages. In other words, you can display Site Targeted ads in these languages only. They are listed below.

| Site Targeted Languages |
| --- |
| ➤ Chinese (Simplified) |
| ➤ Danish |
| ➤ Dutch |
| ➤ English |
| ➤ Finnish |
| ➤ French |
| ➤ German |
| ➤ Hungarian |
| ➤ Italian |
| ➤ Japanese |
| ➤ Korean |
| ➤ Norwegian |
| ➤ Polish |

- ➢ Portuguese
- ➢ Russian
- ➢ Spanish
- ➢ Swedish
- ➢ Turkish

## SITE-RELATED KEYWORDS TAB LANGUAGE

Another way to see which content sites are using your targeted keywords is the Site Related Keywords tabs within the Keywords Tool. This tool, however, is only available to English language preference users.

### d. Onsite Advertiser Sign-Up

When surfing the Web you may have noticed "Advertise on this site" links located usually at the bottom of ad units displayed on Content Network sites.

If you are an AdWords publisher, this link is a powerful tool to enable impressions of your ad on the site. In essence, this link is a Site Target shortcut.

This is how it works. Let's say you offer counseling help for those convicted of DUI (driving while under the influence). The content you have posted on your site is about your services, the dangers of DUI, and various DUI statistics in all 50 of the United States is driving traffic. Your AdWords DUI campaign is also getting clicks and you have seen an increase to the number of opt-ins for your newsletter. You subsequently notice that a prominent law firm in New York, representing clients in various DUI charges, has a great content section that serves up AdSense ads. By clicking on the "Advertise on this site" link on the ad unit, you can target this site for your ads by completing the simple three step sign-up process. In no time your ads will be showing impressions on this New York law firm's site with DUI content as long as your ads will perform better than the worst performing ad in the ad unit.

| **Three Step "Advertise on this site" Sign-Up** |
| --- |
| ➤ Click on the "Advertise on this site" Link;<br>➤ Log Into Your AdWords Account;<br>➤ Complete Three Step Site Targeted Campaign Wizard; |

### 2. Site Sections

Site Sections is a more highly focused version of Site Targeting. With Site Sections you can specify that your ads show on specific pages or even a particular section of a Website within the Content Network.

For example, you may want to pay on a CPM basis for ads shown on a laser hair removal (and very popular) Blog that is industry specific to your laser hair removal machines. Let's also assume that his laser hair removal Blog shows AdSense ads in Wide Skyscraper format down one side and a Wide Rectangle format near the top of the Blog. Knowing that regular readers of this Blog (those contemplating laser hair removal procedures) typically read only the most recent posting, which is at the top of the screen next to the Wide Rectangle unit of AdSense ads focused on laser hair removal, you can target this section of the page to show your ads on a CPM basis. Here you can outsmart your keyword targeting competition who is using a scattershot approach to hopefully get their ads running on the most popular Blog in the laser hair removal industry. Once again, Google provides the tools for smart advertisers to flourish.

## TARGET WEBSITE HOMEPAGES IF RELEVANT

For the vast majority of Websites, the homepage gets the most traffic. Whether through direct traffic or internal clicks once users deep link into a site. Keep this in mind when setting up your Site Sections campaign.

### 3. Sitemaps

With Sitemaps you can easily keep Google updated with any changes made on your site. This is typically used as an AdSense tool so that AdSense publishers can ensure that they will be served the most relevant, content matching ads on a timely basis. As it applies to AdWords campaigns, Sitemaps can act as a powerful keyword tool. Its reporting function tells you the most popular keywords on not only your site, but on all sites that link to yours. This is great way to find keywords that you may not have considered.

With Sitemaps you no longer have wait for the Googlebots to crawl your Web pages for changes to be logged into its site index. Now the Googlebots will be notified when changes occur. They will crawl the exact pages where changes have been made and update it.

## SIGN UP FOR SITEMAPS TODAY

To get your Website registered with Sitemaps for free, visit http://www.google.com/webmasters/sitemaps/login and open your account today.

### a. How to Submit Sitemaps to Google

In fact, you do not need a sitemap at your Web domain to get Google's detailed tracking. When signing up for Sitemaps, Google will ask you if you have a sitemap. If the answer is no, simply input your tracking URL. Google will then generate a unique code that will look something like this: Goog2389djiej38d. To verify you are the owner of the URL so that detailed tracking can begin, Google next requires you to create a .html file with the code as the title (ex., Goog2389djiej38d.html). When you click the "Verify" button, the Googlebots will search the files on your domain server. If the file is there, you will begin receiving detailed stats.

**Three Ways to Submit Sitemaps to Google**

➢ Sitemap Generator
  http://www.google.com/webmasters/sitemaps/docs/en/sitemap-generator.html
➢ XML Sitemap
  http://www.google.com/webmasters/sitemaps/docs/en/protocol.html
➢ Submit a Text File with URLs

### b. Ensure Googlebots Are Not Blocked

With a robots.txt file your Webmaster can inadvertently block Googlebots from searching all or portions of your site. This could skew the keywords being reported to you. How Google does this is by reviewing a robots.txt file located on your domain server. You may not even know you have one. Now Google lets you generate a report that tells you key information about your robots.txt file such as: (1) the last time the Googlebots crawled your site; (2) whether specific URLs within your site are blocking the Googlebot and Google content, image and search crawlers; and (3) test changes your changes.

## TEST ROBOT.TXT CHANGES FIRST

A powerful feature of Sitemaps is the ability to test changes to your robot.txt file *without* modifying it at your Website. See how the various Googlebots and crawlers will react first.

### c. Sitemap Statistics

Another great feature of Google Sitemaps is the built-in statistics tools. It tells you PageRank for all your pages, which search queries are driving traffic to your site, and which pages returned errors such as the dreaded 404 error. Sitemaps also gives detailed stats on searches conducted within Google search and how free traffic based off these searches are finding your site (i.e., what search terms they are using and where your site is ranking for those search results).

## d. Mobile Sitemaps

Google Mobile Sitemaps allows you to submit URLs to the Google index that have been specifically set up for mobile device use such as cellphones and Palm devices.

### MOBILE SITEMAPS FOR WEBMASTERS

Google has very specific rules for mobile Sitemaps. It is highly recommended that you visit http://www.google.com/webmasters/sitemaps/docs/en/mobile.html for the latest information.

## B. Content Network Bid Strategies

It has been demonstrated that clicks on the Content Network are worth much less than clicks on the Search Network primarily because users of the Content Network are not searching for anything. Sure, they may have an interest in a specific article on a particular topic, but that does not mean they are in the market to *buy* a product or service. Their clicks may occur on a whim as they browse through content pages such as when they finish reading a news article. That's why these clicks are worth less and result in a much lower ROI versus an identically priced click on the Search Network. What's more, the number of users clicking on your contextual ad is typically lower than the Click-Through-Rate of search ads due to increased competition from other information on the page. That being said, here is the one-two punch strategy to employ on the Content Network.

### Content Network Bid Strategy

➤ First, drop your Content Network bid by *double* the *difference* in CTR on the Search and Content Networks.

➤ Second, set your Content Network keyword matching to "broad."

In this strategy we are combating the two downsides of the Content Network. By dropping bids on the Content Network you will be able to bring your ROI in line (or in some cases make it much better than) with the Search Network. Next, since it typically takes many more impressions on the Content Network to get a click than on the Search Network, by broadening your keyword match you have made your net that much larger for catching customers.

Here's an example. Let's say you represent clients in Vioxx injury litigation. You are a small law firm of three aggressive lawyers who focus on alleged damages from Vioxx related heart attacks. On the Search Network you create Ad Groups and specific ads for all COX-2 drugs on the market.

**Title Line:**      Vioxx Lawsuits
**Bodyline1:**      Aggressive Law Firm Will
**Bodyline2:**      Represent Your Vioxx Injury Claim.
**URL Line:**       [Website].com

Your maximum CPC is $0.10. You find that your CTR is around 1.5% on the Search Network. On the Content Network you are getting ten times the number of impressions, but your CTR is a mere 0.3% or $1/5^{th}$ of what it is on the Search Network. Dropping your Content Network bid by *double* this amount $(1/10^{th})$, you will be getting roughly the same amount of click traffic at half the cost as on the Search Network. The problem still exists, however, that once Content Network users reach your site, they are less likely to buy than Search Network users. To remedy this shortfall, you must get *more* clicks from the Content Network.

It may appear that the best way to accomplish this is to broaden your keyword matching on the Content Network, but Google does not allow keyword matching for the Content Network.

## NO KEYWORD MATCHING ON THE CONTENT NETWORK

Keyword matching does not apply to AdWords ads selected to show in Google's Content Network. The Traffic Estimator Tool controls keyword matching.

## Traffic Estimator

Get quick traffic estimates for new keywords without adding them to an account or using the AdWo

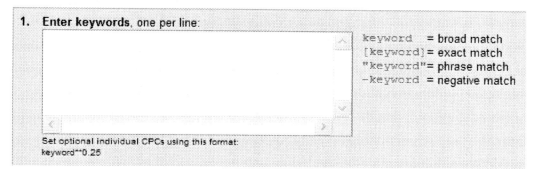

All is not lost, however. A great way to get more clicks on the Content Network is to use Google's Site Targeting Tool to focus on your ads on content sites popular with the audience you want to reach.

## All Campaigns
✚ Create a new campaign: keyword-targeted | site-targeted [?]

In this example we would focus on sites running AdSense ads and that content for finding Vioxx attorneys. We would even run ads with common spellings of the drug like "Viox attorneys" and "Viox lawyers." We would also target Vioxx drug recall sites where users of the drug may visit. And best of all, you could get these clicks for $0.01. If the ads are written correctly, you should be able to increase your impressions on the Content Network and limit the amount of bad clicks.

### C. Click Fraud
Click fraud occurs when an Internet user clicks on an ad with no

intention of purchasing the underlying product or service. Click fraud is a growing problem in the Pay-Per-Click industry. There are instances of "Clickbots" or "Hitbots" being programmed to automatically click on competitor ads. Here are the three forms click fraud takes.

## 1. Publisher Clicks

Publishers on the Content Network may be tempted to click on AdSense ads showing on their own Websites since Google shares in click revenue with them. If Google detects this type of click fraud it will not share any revenue with the Website owner and will not charge you, the AdWord advertiser, a CPC. Here are all the instances where Google will not share revenue or charge you a CPC for AdSense ads.

### Five Instances of No CPC Being Charged

"Google shall not be liable for any payment based on (a) any amounts which result from invalid queries, or invalid clicks on Ads generated by any person, bot, automated program or similar device, including, without limitation, through any clicks or impressions (i) originating from Your IP addresses or computers under Your control, or (ii) solicited by payment of money, false representation or request for users to click on Ads; (b) Ads delivered to end users whose browsers have JavaScript disabled; (c) Ads benefiting charitable organizations and other placeholder or transparent Ads that Google may deliver; (d) Google advertisements for its own products and/or services; or (e) clicks co-mingled with a significant number of invalid clicks described in (a) above, or as a result of any breach of this Agreement by You for any applicable pay period."

## 2. Advertiser Clicks

Increasing CTR is important in AdWords. The obvious solution may appear that you should click on your *own* ad to get its CTR up. This, however, is a losing strategy and is click fraud. The first AdWords Commandment is "Thou shalt not click on thine own ad." Not only will you be wasting your own advertising money, you are merely putting a bandage on an injured ad that really needs stitches. This quick fix will not solve the ultimate issues with your ad. Either the ad itself is of low quality or you have targeted the wrong keywords.

## 3. Competitor Clicks

A more rampant problem exists where competitors may click on your AdWord ads to run up your advertising costs. If you suspect this is happening in your industry, here are some of the leading click fraud prevention companies and their URLs.

---

### Click Fraud Detection & Prevention Companies

- ClickFacts – Free click fraud detection if you display ClickFacts button on Website; www.clickfacts.com
- Clicklab – Multiple criteria to spot fraud; www.clicklab.com
- PPCTrax.com – Offers various click fraud packages; www.ppctrax.com
- WhosClickingWho – After five or more repeated clicks from the same URL a pop-up blocker sends a warning; www.whosclickingwho.com

---

## D. Prescription Drugs and Related Content

Websites seeking to advertise online prescription drugs or for those that target prescription drug keywords in the U.S. Country Region, a valid SquareTrade identification number must be provided to Google.

## SQUARE TRADE MEMBERSHIPS

> Only online pharmacies based in the U.S. or Canada may receive a SquareTrade membership. International online pharmacies may not include the U.S. within their Google Country Region. Visit www.SquareTrade.com to get your seal today.

Here is a link to Google's Online Pharmacy Qualification Program. Http://www.google.com/adwords/pharmacy_qualification.html.

## ONLINE PHARMACY QUALIFICATION PROGRAM EXCEPTIONS

> If you do not believe that Google's Online Pharmacy Qualification Program is applicable to your Website, you may request an exception for a particular ad or keyword from Google's editors while creating your ad online.

## X. Examples of Crucial Advertising Dos and Don'ts

Below are examples of searches covering business-to-business and business-to-consumer markets. In particular, examples are shown for the consumer electronics industry, travel services, real estate services, consumer services, consumer products and the personal services industry, which are common for small businesses. Here we will dissect representative ads in these marketing campaigns and show good and bad advertising practices. Many are common for small businesses. Before we start, let's take a look at the top twenty-five advertising hooks used to attract purchasers. You will also note how so few of the advertisers profiled used these tricks.

### Top 25 Advertising Hooks

1. Buy one, get one free
2. Car rental discounts
3. Car rental upgrades
4. Coupon with purchase
5. Discount on multiple purchases
6. Dollar discounts
7. Entry into sweepstakes with purchase
8. Free accessory
9. Free club membership
10. Free expedited shipping
11. Free gift card
12. Free gift with purchase
13. Free gift wrapping
14. Free shipping
15. Free upgrade
16. Frequent flier miles
17. Hotel discounts
18. Percentage discounts
19. Percentage of sale donated to charity
20. Rebate

21. Secret
22. Tips
23. Tricks
24. Hints
25. Specials

| Google Search | Psychology Degree Online |

Sponsored Links

**Online Psychology** Degrees
Find and compare psych/counseling
degrees in a directory of programs.
[Website].com

Two of three search terms matched in
Title. Bodylines form one sentence.
"compare" draws attention. All words
not capitalized in Bodylines.

**Psychology** Courses
**Psychology** Courses At [School]
Learn From Home - Free Catalog!
www.[Website].edu

"Psychology" starts Bodylines &
Title. All words capitalized. "Free
Catalog" draws attention.

Univ. of [School] **Online**
America's leading **online** university
since 1976. Learn more today.
www.[Website].info

Only one search term matched in the
Title. "Psychology" & "Degreee" not
used anywhere in ad. "Learn more
today" is good call to action.

[School] **Online Degree**
Earn a [School] **degree online**
Grad/Undergrad programs available
www.[Website].edu

Two of three search terms matched in
Title and Bodylines. Good info about
"Grad/Undergrad program" being
available.

## AFFILIATE WEBSITES

"Affiliate" Websites are those being paid to redirect visitors to
another Website or distributor. Google shows one affiliate ad per
search and at most two ads from the same Website. A search for
"Entire Tales & Poems of Edgar Allan Poe" will cause Google to
inventory its Affiliate ads for those keywords and display only the
most relevant ad.

Google Search | Traveling Agency

Sponsored Links

Find Flights
SuperSearch Across Multiple
Airline Sites For Low Fares
www.[website].com

Title not directly related to keywords. Bodylines flow as one sentence, but no punctuation. No keywords bolded. Ad does little to stand apart.

Travel **Agency**
[Brand]: The Faster, Easier Way to
Find Travel **Agency** Travel Deals!
www.[Brand].com

One keyword in Title and Bodylines. "Easier" and "Deals" draw attention. Good brand recognition in ad and use of capital letters.

Travel **Agency**
Find listings of Travel Agents
in your area – [Brand].com
www.[Brand].com

Only one keyword in Title. Good brand recognition in ad and use of capital letters. Not as good as Ad #2.

Travel **Agency**
Shop and Compare Great Deals on
Flights, Hotels, Cars and Packages.
www.[Website].com

One keyword in Title only. Bodylines convey breadth of product offering.

## REGISTER SMART DOMAIN NAMES

Create content and register domain names with your product. The link will be to your Website not an affiliated site. This means that smart advertisers will be rewarded and those merely serving as a pass-through to another site will get overlooked.

| Google Search | Auto Insurance Quotes |

Sponsored Links

**[Company] Auto Insurance**
How Much Could You Save?
Get a Free **Auto Insurance** Quote!
www.[Website].com

Title has two of the keywords. Question draws attention as does "Free." Nice ad.

**Auto Insurance Quotes**
Comparison Shop Tennessee Rates.
Fast & Free Unbeatable Online Rates
www.[Website].com
Tennessee

Keywords are the Title! "Fast & Free" draws attention. Great use of Tennessee state market. Best ad.

**[Company] Auto Insurance**
Save Up to $300 by Dealing Direct!
Get a Free Instant Quote Online.
www.[Website].com

Title has two of the keywords. "Free Instant Quote" draws attention, but ad #1 is better by using two of the keywords to get the same message across.

**Need Car Insurance Quotes**
Compare **quotes** from top providers
in just 5 minutes! - 1-888-868-1234
www.[website]l.com
Tennessee

Title would have been better with a question mark at end. Great use of telephone number in ad. Numbers jump out.

## NO DIALER ADS

Dialer ads are not allowed. Dialers are switching software that change a modem's dial tone used to access the Internet to a long distance number that is billed to the Internet user. It comes as no surprise that Google does not permit ads associated with dialers or dialer software in any way.

| Google Search | Incorporating in Florida |

Sponsored Links

**Incorporating** in **Florida**
Easy Low Cost **Florida** Incorporation
Save time & money at [Website].com
www.[Website].com

Title matches keywords. Lots of great words draw attention like "Easy Low Cost" and "Save time & money." Words not capitalized on Bodyline 2.

Incorporate in **Florida**
Form a Corporation or LLC. Fast, easy, low-cost. Trusted since 1976!
www.[Website].com

Title could have easily included all keywords. Good words to draw attention and show duration of business.

Incorporate Your Business
Quick, simple, and guaranteed.
1-888-692-6771 for live help.
www.[Website].com

No keywords bolded in ad. Great use of toll free telephone number to make ad stand out.

Incorporate in **Florida**
Fast, Professional, Low Prices.
Featured in USA Today and on CNN.
www.[Website].com

Title could have easily included all keywords. Use of USA Today and CNN draw attention.

## COMMON WORDS NEVER BOLDED

Google will not bold common words such as "the, and, or, in, of" even if they are included as a keyword. This prevents ads from including too many bolded words.

| Google Search | Equity Loan Bad Credit |

Sponsored Links

**Bad Credit** Home **Equity**
Free home **equity** quotes from up to
4 lenders. One quick, easy form.
www.[Website].com

Three of four keywords in Title. Only one keyword in Bodylines. Words "Free," "quick," and "easy," standout.

[Company]: Home **Equity**
Get Up to 125% of Your Home's Value
4 out of 5 Applicants Approved!
www.[Website].com

Only one of four keywords used in entire ad! Good use of numbers to make text stand out.

**Bad Credit Equity Loan**
$170,000 **Loan** as low as $560/month
Up to 4 free quotes. Intro terms
[Website].com
Tennessee

Best ad. All keywords used as Title. Great use of numbers and pricing.

**Equity loan**
No Lenders Fees. Fast Application.
Low Rates. **Bad Credit** Okay.
www.[Website].biz

Only two of four keywords in Title and "loan" not capitalized. Good use of compelling words.

## BE CAREFUL OF LANDING PAGE

If your ad has a price, special discount, "free," or "giveaway" language, it must be clearly and accurately displayed on your Website within one or two clicks of the page on which customers land after clicking on your ad.

| Google Search | Tax Attorney |

Sponsored Links

**Tax** Relief **Attorney**
Don't be Afraid of the IRS Anymore.
Save Money - Get **Tax** Relief Fast!
[Website].com

Both keywords used in Title, but just "Tax Attorney" may be better. "Tax Relief Fast" draws attention. Good elimination of www before URL name.

Expert **Tax** Attorneys
Immediately Stop Wage Garnishments
**Tax** Levies, Reduce Taxes 95% & More
www.[Website].org

Plural on "Attorneys" in Title keeps it from being bolded. Good use of numbers to make ad stand out.

**Tax Attorney**
We Solve **Tax** Problems
IRS Problems, Audit, **Tax** Court
www.[Website].net

Keywords *are* the Title! No mention of garnishment, but otherwise good statement of services.

Nationwide **Tax** Lawyers
Nationwide directory of attorneys &
law firms specializing in **Tax** Law.
www.[Website].com

Only one keyword used in Title. No numbers in Bodylines to draw attention. "Nationwide" gives ad a large scope of reach.

## ONLINE GAMBLING ADS ALLOWED

Google now allows AdWord ads for online gambling. This includes online casinos, sports books, bingo, and affiliates with the primary purpose of driving traffic to online gambling sites.

## XI. Overlooked Google Advertising Programs

### A. Froogle

Since this book is about advertising on Google, it would be remiss without including Google's dedicated shopping site called Froogle (pronounced "Frugal"). Froogle is fast becoming one of the Internet's premier shopping comparison sites. When potential customers search for a product within Froogle, a list of products are shown along with description and pricing information. Thumbnail photos of the product are also included. What's best about Froogle is that it is totally free! That's right. As long as you meet the simple guidelines, there is neither a minimum-spending amount nor a charge for clicks. There isn't even a registration fee. Visit www.froogle.com and get your free advertising campaign started today!

### FROOGLE ADWORDS CLICK CHARGES

> Froogle is part of Google's Internal Search Network. AdWord clicks are charged at the normal CPC that you have specified.

In addition, AdWord ads are displayed in two different ways next to products. The first is in the right hand column next to search results.

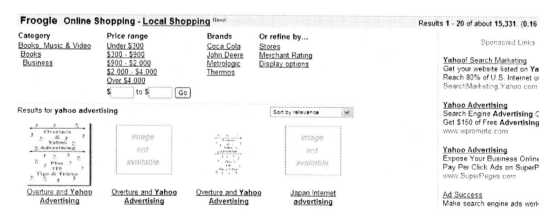

The second instance when AdWord ads are displayed on Froogle is when a particular product is clicked on. A dedicated page opens showing a picture of the item (when available) along with purchasing information. Ad units containing three AdWord ads are shown across the top and bottom of the page.

**Yahoo! Search Marketing**
Get your website listed on Yahoo!
Reach 80% of U.S. Internet users.
SearchMarketing.Yahoo.com

**Yahoo Advertising**
Search Engine Advertising Campaigns
Get $150 of Free Advertising Today!
www.wpromote.com

**Yahoo Advertising**
Expose Your Business Online with
Pay Per Click Ads on SuperPages
www.SuperPages.com

**Overture and Yahoo Advertising: Plus 110 Tips and Tricks by Bottletree Books**

Price: **$10.65 - $28.41**

Description from Booksamillion.com: Club Price: $14.83. Free U.S. shipping with $25 order. Save on Overture and Yahoo Advertising: Plus 110 Tips and Tricks at Books-A-Million.

## NO FROOGLE SHARING OF CLICK CHARGES

Unlike AdSense and Google Books, there is no sharing of click revenue on Froogle.

### B. Google Catalogs

Google provides yet another free way for you to advertise. It's called Google Catalogs. Under this service Google's leading search technology is used on thousands of scanned mail order catalogs. All you have to do to get your product catalog included is to mail it to Google.

## VISIT GOOGLE CATALOGS TODAY

To search Google Catalogs simply visit www.catalogs.google.com

### Catalogs

Desantis Collection
Page 1 of 96
... Name GOOGLE CATALOGS 1 ...
[ More results from this catalog ]

Brigade Quartermasters
Page 225 of 274
... , SG-1 V-Cut (Extra Ventilation) Goggles • $8999 WILEY X® COC TACTICAL GOOGLE
This new full ...
[ More results from this catalog ]

---

### How to Add Your Catalog on Google

- ➢ Add Google to your catalog mailing list;
- ➢ Use this address: **Google Catalogs**
    **171 Main Street, #280A**
    **Los Altos, CA 94022**
    **USA**
- ➢ Send a notification email to: Catalog-Vendors@Google.com once Google is added to your mailing list; and
- ➢ Your catalog will be scanned by Google and placed on its Website within a few days after Google receives it.

---

## NO ADS IN GOOGLE CATALOGS

At present no AdWord ads are displayed for Google Catalog search results or when the catalog is displayed.

## C. Zeitgeist

Determining what products and services are of interest on the Internet can be difficult for most advertisers. This illusive and ever changing information is essential for a successful Internet marketing campaign. It would take an army of data collection agents to gather this information. Nothing to fear. Google provides yet another free, but relatively little used tool that gathers this information for you. It is called Zeitgeist, which is translated "Time Spirit" and can be found at www.google.com/press/zeitgeist.html.

### NO ADS IN ZEIGEIST

At present no AdWord ads are displayed for Google Zeitgeist buzz results.

Google's Zeitgeist provides the following most popular search category data:

### Zeitgeist Popular Search Results

1. Top Image Search Queries
2. Popular TV Shows
3. Popular Text Queries
4. Popular Athletes
5. Popular Men
6. Popular Women
7. Popular Movies
8. Popular Cities
9. Popular Animals
10. Popular News Organizations
11. Popular Airlines
12. Popular Beauty-Related Queries
13. Popular Google News Queries

14. Top Political Queries
15. Top Retailers
16. Top 10 Gaining
17. Top 10 Declining

## ZEITGEIST BUZZ TIPS

If you run a traveling agency, use the Zeitgeist Popular Cities and Popular Airlines results to target your marketing campaign. If your business is in the multibillion dollar a year cosmetic field, the Zeitgeist Popular Beauty-Related Queries data is a must. There are no limits to how Google's free marketing data can be used.

Google provides data on the above popular searches in the following countries. Each is hyperlinked for your convenience.

### Zeitgeist Countries

1. Australia - www.google.com.au/press/zeitgeist.html
2. Brazil - www.google.com.br/press/zeitgeist.html
3. Canada - www.google.ca/press/zeitgeist.html
4. Chile - www.google.cl/press/zeitgeist.html
5. Denmark - www.google.dk/press/zeitgeist.html
6. Finland - www.google.fi/press/zeitgeist.html
7. France - www.google.fr/press/zeitgeist.html
8. Germany - www.google.de/press/zeitgeist.html
9. India – www.google.co.in/press/zeitgeist.html
10. Ireland – www.google.ie/press/zeitgeist.html
11. Israel – www.google.co.il/press/zeitgeist.html
12. Italy - www.google.it/press/zeitgeist.html
13. Japan - www.google.co.jp/press/zeitgeist.html
14. Korea - www.google.co.kr/press/zeitgeist.html

15. Netherlands - www.google.nl/press/zeitgeist.html
16. New Zealand – www.google.co.nz/press/zeitgeist.html
17. Poland – www.google.pl/press/zeitgeist.html
18. Russia - www.google.ru/press/zeitgeist.html
19. Spain - www.google.es/press/zeitgeist.html
20. Sweden - www.google.se/press/zeitgeist.html
21. Turkey – www.google.com.tr/press/zeitgeist.html
22. United Kingdom - www.google.co.uk/press/zeitgeist.html
23. United States - www.google.com/press/zeitgeist.html
24. Vietnam – www.google.com.vn/press/zeitgeist.html

## ZEITGEIST YOUR FOREIGN MARKETING CAMPAIGN

Zeitgeist provides one-year data on the various languages used to access Google. Use this free data to further tailor your marketing campaign such that ads are not only created for various regions but also languages within those regions.

## D. Gmail

### 1. Introduction

In 2004 Google introduced the world to its new email program called Gmail. Under this free and evolutionary email program, Google computers scan email messages for keywords and phrases. Google inserts AdWords text alongside the email message using the same contextual advertising technology it uses for AdSense. Gmail users then click on these ads from within their email messages to buy your products or services. This is yet another market for your Google advertising campaign.

## NO IMAGE ADS IN GMAIL

At present, Gmail only displays text ads next to email messages. No Image Ads are permitted.

## 2. Gmail Ad Structure

There are two ways AdWords ads are shown in the millions of Gmail messages that are displayed every day. We'll explore both below.

### a. Inbox: RSS Feeds Across the Top

Any time a Gmail user uses the features of its Inbox, Google displays RSS feeds across the top of the screen.

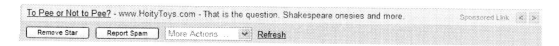

The Gmail user selects what feeds will be shown across the top from a variety of Web content sites such as Forbes and Yahoo. New RSS feeds are displayed in two ways. First, Gmail users can flip to a new feed using the arrows on the right of the RSS feed bar or second, each time a Gmail user selects a new Inbox section such as "Sent Mail," "Spam," or "Trash," a new RSS feed is shown across the top of the screen.

AdWord ads are also shown in the RSS feed line. The ads shown are top-ranking ads, and this provides yet another avenue for you to get clicks on the internal Google Content Network. As you will see above, the ad Title is shown with hyphens delineating the displayed URL. The Body of the ad follows. This bifurcation of Title and Body is yet another reason for you not to make the Title and Body one long sentence.

## AdWord RSS Feeds Cannot be Disabled

Gmail users can disable any or all of the RSS content feeds, but they cannot disable AdWord ads from being shown across the top of Gmail Inboxes.

You may wonder how RSS AdWord ads are triggered? They are triggered off the *first* title within the particular Inbox segment. For example, if the first title of an email message in your "Sent Mail" segment includes the words "Yahoo Advertising," then the ad with the highest Quality Score that is bidding on the keywords "Yahoo Advertising" will be displayed when the Gmail user clicks over to the "Sent Mail" segment.

### b. Email Message: Right-Hand Column Ads

The primary way ads are shown in Gmail is down the right-hand side of the page when an email message is opened. News information and map directions (if there is an address in the email messge) are also shown. Here is an example of a column of ads and news information that run alongside an email message received in a Gmail account. Let's analyze each section shown next to a Gmail message.

The Sponsored Links section shows a maximum of 4 AdWords ads next to the opened email message. They are triggered off keywords within the email.

Titles are also scanned. If a Gmail message is sent with only a title and no text in the body, which is common in cases where only an email attachment is being sent, ads will trigger based upon keywords in the *title* of the email.

Deference is given to keywords in the body of the email message over keywords in the title.

Large Arial 12 point font is used for the AdWord Titles in Sponsored Links within Gmail.

Within the "Related Pages" section of Gmail advertising, two Google news segments are displayed below the Sponsored Links section.

These are non-paid news articles.

Arial 10 point font is used for the news article titles. Note that some extend to three lines, unlike the AdWords Titles that are only one line.

Sponsored Links

## Miles For Cash
We pay money for miles & frequent flyer points on all airlines.
www.[website].com

## OPT Rewards Secrets
Learn membership benefits & secrets. Earn business class upgrades
www.[website].com

## XYZ Airlines ® site
Now with our Best Fare Guarantee. Book today and save at website.com!
www.[website].com

## Frequent Flyer Miles
Get 100,000 points in a year. Learn how today!
www.[website].com

**more sponsored links »**

Related Pages
Continental Airlines offers Flights to New York from Hong Kong for ...
ASIATravelTips.com -
10 hours ago
Continental Airlines in Hong Kong has launched special fares or ...

Collect miles all over China with Air China Partnership extended ...
noticias.info - 28 minutes ago
/noticias.info/ As of now, travellers to China have even more ...

At the bottom on the Related Pages section is displayed information from two Websites.

Up to three lines are displayed for the Website title and three lines for the Website explanation.

Arial 10 point font is used for the news article titles.

Discount First Class Airfare, Business Class Airfare ...
Access Fares offers discount airline tickets to travellers for both ...
www.[website].com

Airline Miles for Sale - Buy Frequent Flyer Miles - Delta SkyMiles ...
Buy Frequent Flyer Miles as a Gift or to complete a free ticket
www.[website].com

more related pages »

Since Google's software algorithms insert AdWord ads next to the text of email messages, it raises the question whether these ads "stick" with the message or whether new ads are displayed each time the email message is opened and read. No stickiness here. Google scans each email every time it is opened and inserts updated Sponsored Links and Related Pages. If ads did stick within Gmail, a user could open an email that is 6 months old and click on an ad that may no longer be operational or create click charges for an advertiser that has stopped showing ads.

## NO ADS SHOWN WHEN EMAIL PRINTED

When a user prints an email message from Gmail, no Sponsored Links or Related Pages information is printed beside the message.

### E.    Google Book Search

### 1. Introduction

Google also introduced Google Print in 2004, which allows book publishers to have their books scanned into electronic format and partially displayed when a searcher types in a keyword or phrase contained in the book. This includes copies of old books housed in university libraries that are long out of circulation. In 2005 they changed the name to Google Book Search. Now, what does this mean for you as a Google advertiser? It is yet another place where your ads are displayed.

### 2. Google Book Search Ad Structure

There are two ways in which AdWord ads are served on Google Book Search and we will explore each below.

### a. Search Results: Right-Hand Column

The first place your ads will be shown is when a search for a term or title is conducted on Google Book Search. Down the left-hand side of the results page will be shown thumbnail book covers containing that term or title and down the right-hand side of the page will be AdWords text ads. If these ads are clicked on, no revenue is shared with the publishers.

### b. Page Impressions: Bottom of Page

Second, when one of the book thumbnails is clicked on and the portion of the book containing the search term is displayed, your ad is shown *below* the book results. If your ad is clicked on, Google shares the click payment with the book publisher under its Google Books

Partner Program. Similar to the AdSense program, the percentage that is shared is secret. The great thing is that this revenue sharing comes out of Google's own pocket. You do not have to pay more for these clicks even though Google is getting less revenue. Just as with Gmail, Image Ads are not displayed alongside book results, only text ads.

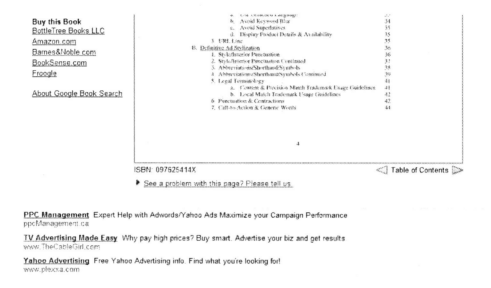

PPC Management Expert Help with Adwords/Yahoo Ads Maximize your Campaign Performance
ppcManagement.ca

TV Advertising Made Easy Why pay high prices? Buy smart. Advertise your biz and get results
www.TheCableGirl.com

Yahoo Advertising Free Yahoo Advertising info. Find what you're looking for!
www.plexxa.com

### VISIT GOOGLE BOOK SEARCH TODAY

You can try out Google Book Search at www.books.google.com and receive the latest Book Search information.

## F. Google Video

### 1. Introduction

In 2005 Google Video was launched, which enables individuals and companies to upload digital video onto Google's servers free of charge. Users, such as family members, can then download home movies. On the commercial front, Google Video Store users can download or rent videos on demand from content owners and creators. This includes large movie and television studios. Non-commercial items posted on Google Video that may soon be supported by AdWord ads, while commercial content is typically a pay-to-download or a pay-to-own service.

### SIGN UP FOR GOOGLE VIDEO TODAY

Google Video can be found on the Web at www.Video.Google.com where you can sign up for free.

## 2. Google Video Structure

Google Video is relatively new. It provides a great way for you to advertise your products and services on the Web using video.

### a. Search Results

Users have three searching options. The first is by using a "Search Video" box at the top of the screen. "Popular" clips are shown on the front page, which can be clicked on and viewed in their entirety. Users can also select the "Random" tab to learn what's new and arbitrary in videos on the service.

### b. Video Playback

You can also focus in on videos being uploaded from a particular area of the country by zip code. This way you can zero in on certain areas with many video producers such as Los Angeles or New York. Google sets the default as 94043, which is the zip code for Mountain View, California. This just happens to be the worldwide headquarters for Google, by the way. At time of publication, local TV shows are only available in the United States, but expect this to change soon.

Just as with Google Books and AdSense, Google plans to shares an undisclosed percentage of each AdWord click with video content owners. This is a great marketing opportunity if you own or create video content and will soon be yet another market for AdWord ads. At this time, however, ads are not displayed.

All this begs the question: Since AdWord ads are triggered on keywords, how does Google search video to know which ads should be shown next to what video? Well, underlying each video is a wealth of text data that Google searches to link ads. Here is the text data available for keyword linking.

| **Google Video Text Searching Items** |
| --- |
| Television Videos<br>➢ Titles<br>➢ Closed Captioning<br><br>Non-Television Videos<br>➢ Titles |

> ➢ Metadata (Video Overviews; Place Created; Date Created; Director; Actors)

### G.    Google Base

### 1. Introduction

Launched in 2005, Google Base is best described as a free classified ads database containing everything from comic books to cars. This is one of the first Google databases that contains set forms to allow people to input "searchable" items. Like most Google programs, it is offered free of charge and Google will host the information for you (also free of charge). With Google Base you do not even need a Website.

### ENTER YOUR PRODUCTS TODAY

To get started with Google Base visit www.base.google.com and input your data today.

### 2. Google Base Structure

Google Base is actually a living, breathing online database that adapts to the popularity of items inputted and the attributes selected within its Items.

### ONLY AVAILABLE IN ENGLISH?

Google Base is supposedly only available in English, but we have noticed postings in French, Spanish and Portuguese.

**Put Stuff on Google**

Google Base is a place where you can post all types of content and have it show up on Google. Learn more: FAQ, Google Base blog

Andy.Barger@gmail.com's items

## Post your own item

### Post multiple items with a bulk upload file

**Recent Searches**
beetle
dance
honda civic
engineering jobs
cancer
pumpkin pie recipe
java

**Browse posted items**

| | | | |
|---|---|---|---|
| Blogs | Mobile Content | Protein databases | Rentals |
| Coupons | News and articles | Products | Services |
| Events and activities | Patents | Recipes | Vehicles |

## a. Items

Here are the current stock Items for inputting on Google Base or your can create your own Item.

| Fifteen Different Google Base Items |
|---|
| ➢ Course Schedules |
| ➢ Custom Item |
| ➢ Events & Activities |
| ➢ Jobs |
| ➢ News & Articles |
| ➢ People Profiles |
| ➢ Products |
| ➢ Recipes |
| ➢ Reference Articles |
| ➢ Reviews |
| ➢ Services |
| ➢ Travel Packages |
| ➢ Vehicles |

> ➢ Want Ads

## b. Attributes

What separates Google Base from most online databases is that you can assign multiple attributes to your listings within each category. For instance, when listing a product you include such attributes as "Color," "Make," "Author," "ISBN," etc. to help users find you.

At present Google Base does not show AdWord ads next to the search results, but this could change in the future. We have included this section on Google Base to show you another free and powerful advertising venue for you on Google. If your item is popular on Google Base, Google may even add it to its internal Google Search Network results.

### SIGN UP FOR THE GOOGLE BASE BLOG

Get the latest Google Base news by signing up for its Blog at http://googlebase.blogspot.com/

## XII. Tools to Analyze Your Advertising Campaign

We have discussed the most effective ways to start your advertising campaign on Google and how to use its basket of ad optimize tools to gain the most clicks at the lowest Cost-Per-Click. Now we will survey the various analyzation and management tools available under the appropriately titled "Campaign Management" tab for tracking who is visting your site, what they are doing while there, and what ads are converting new customers. Effective use of these tools and techniques will make your advertising campaign on Google that much more of a success.

Google provides a fantastic set of *free* tools to analyze every aspect of your campaign's performance. We'll discuss each below.

---

### Six Tools to Analyze Your Ads

➤ Analytics Tool
➤ Ads Diagnostic Tool
➤ Conversion Tracking Tool
➤ Destination URL Tool
➤ Disapproved Ads Tool
➤ My Change History Tool

---

### A. Analytics Tool

Google Analytics acts very much like the Conversion Tracking Tool below. Think of it as the Conversion Tracking Tool on steroids. Once again Google has provided a very powerful and *free* tool to track all aspects of user activities on your site and even how they got there.

Google Analytics is so versatile we assume it will soon replace Conversion Tracking, but for now you have both tools at your disposal.

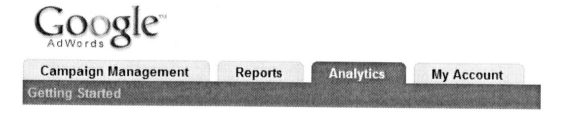

The interest in Google Analytics was so overwhelming when it was first introduced, Google had to limit its access. Even if you are not using Conversion Tracking, we highly recommend Google Analytics. It takes only a few minutes to set up.

**How to Enable Google Analytics**

1. Select the "Analytics" tab within AdWords
2. Sign up
3. Add tracking code to HTML of your Website
4. Select tracking goal
5. Select path through your Website to ultimate conversion
6. Select "Enable Tracking Codes" button in AdWords

### VISIT THE GOOGLE ANALYTICS HELP FORUM

Get the latest Analytics help and discuss Analytics best practices with other users at http://groups.google.com/group/analytics-help

### B. Ads Diagnostic Tool

With the powerful Ads Diagnostics Tool, you can learn when impressions of your ads are showing and for what keywords, and what position they rank in AdWords.

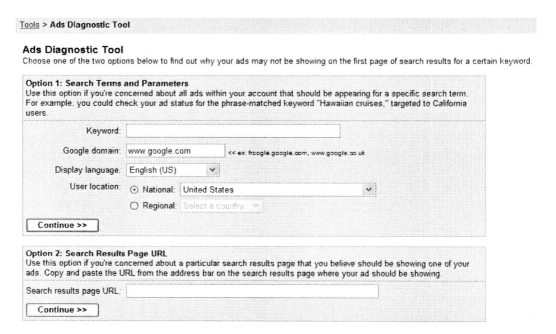

Like the rest of the ad analyzation tools, the Ads Diagnostic Tool is found under the Tools tab.

### C. Conversion Tracking Tool

You can use the Conversion Tracking Tool to learn which ads are performing the best *and* getting you the most sales or opt-ins. Conversion Tracking is displayed on the Campaign Summary page.

| Campaign Management | Reports | Analytics | My Account |
|---|---|---|---|

Campaign Summary | Tools | Conversion Tracking

## ANOTHER REASON TO ENABLE CONVERSION TRACKING

Google's Smart Pricing adjusts your CPC lower on the Content Network if clicks are not getting "business results," including revenues, email list registrations, clicks on AdSense advertisements, newsletter signups, etc. But you (and especially not Google) will not know this unless you have Conversion Tracking enabled.

## 1. Channel Tracking

Think of channel tracking as your click-to-purchase watchdog. Google provides conversion tracking html code that you simply cut and paste into the html code of your Website. The code is placed on the "Thank You" page that is shown after a user has purchased from your Website so that Google can track use from click-to-purchase and inform you which keywords are successful in your campaign. Note that Google places the following text "Google Site Stats" on your "Thank You" page to alert users that their purchase has been tracked. Google includes this notification to users as part of its Privacy Policy. The conversion text block itself is customizable to your particular Website.

### Two Conversion Tracking Options

1. Pause or Make Active Conversion Tracking
2. Get Conversion Tracking Code - Here Google provides the actual code you copy into the HTML of your Website for this

tracking. Visit https://adwords.google.com/select/setup.pdf to view Google's helpful Conversion Tracking Guide, which is in .pdf format.

## SET UP A SEPARATE CAMPAIGN FOR EACH CHANNEL

Similar to how you should create an Ad Group for each unique product you sell, create a Campaign for each channel (i.e., URL).

## 2. Cross-Channel Tracking

This technical-sounding term "cross-channel tracking," is merely a way for you to track other Internet advertising campaigns such as those on Yahoo. The Cross-Channel Tracking Tool allows you to monitor all campaigns from your AdWords account and to compare which ones are getting you the best ROI. By providing this free tool Google is betting that your best result will come from AdWords. Regardless, you can use the detailed tracking tools to make the best decisions about where your Internet advertising money is being spent. Here are the steps to enable cross-channel tracking.

### Steps to Setting Up Cross-Channel Tracking

➢ Choose a Pay-Per-Click or Non-Pay-Per-Click Channel;
➢ Create a Campaign for this Channel;
➢ Insert Google's code into the landing page of your Website;
➢ Take auto-generated URLs Google provides when creating your Campaign and make them the URLs for your Campaign ads (these should be the linking URLs, *not* the URLs displayed when impressions of your ad are shown); and
➢ Get conversion data for all your cross-channels in one place.

## SET UP A SEPARATE CAMPAIGN FOR EACH CROSS-CHANNEL

Similar to how you should create an Ad Group for each unique product you sell, create a Campaign for each cross-channel (i.e., Non-Google advertising campaign.

### D. Destination URLs

A little-used tool for tracking clicks on the Search and Content Networks is to designate a unique Destination URL for your keywords (i.e., the URL to where potential customers will be taken after clicking on your ad). Google calls this ValueTrack and it allows you to place a Fast Track Tag onto the end of your Destination URLs for this tracking.

| The Destination URL Code |
| --- |
| www.[yourwebsite].com?type={ifsearch:GoogleAdWordsSearch}{ifcontent:GoogleAdWordsContent} |

This is a good tool if you do wish to run cross-channel tracking, yet have multiple non-Google PPC advertising campaigns such as one on Yahoo or Kanoodle. By using the Destination URL code, Weblogs on your domain name hosting company will display clicks from the Google Search Network as:

**www.[yourwebsite].com?type=GoogleAdWordsSearch**

and for the Google Content Network, clicks will be reported as:

**www.[yourwebsite].com?type=GoogleAdWordsContent**

ValueTrack does not provide conversion tracking. It only provides limited click tracking that tells you in a general sense whether the ad click came from the Google Search Network, Google Content

Network, or an organic click. Since Google already tracks the number of clicks received on each network, Destination URLs are of little value. You will get much better insight into the click and buying patterns of your Website users by implementing Conversion Tracking or Google Analytics.

### E. Disapproved Ads

Okay. There are some times when your submitted ads get rejected and you need to know the reasons why. There is no greater waste of time on AdWords than adding new ads based on ones that have already been rejected . . . which means the new ads will likewise be rejected. Use this tool to learn *why* Google's editors disapproved your rejected ads *before* writing new ones.

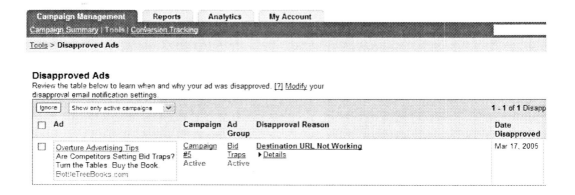

## THE #1 REASON WHY ADS GET REJECTED

> The most common reason why Google's editors turn down ads is a non-working URL link. Make sure this is working before adding new ads and save yourself time.

### F. Change History Tool

Google has created a very useful tool that allows you to find the date when you made nearly any change within your AdWords campaign over the past three months. The Change History Tool is, intuitively, located on the Tools page of your account. One of its best uses is to look back in time and learn what changes to your account resulted in more clicks or higher sales.

## CHANGE HISTORY TOOL IS GREAT FOR MANAGED ACCOUNTS

If you have multiple people within your organization or your AdWords account is managed by an outside service, the Change History Tool will allow those people to see when a change a change was made and who made it.

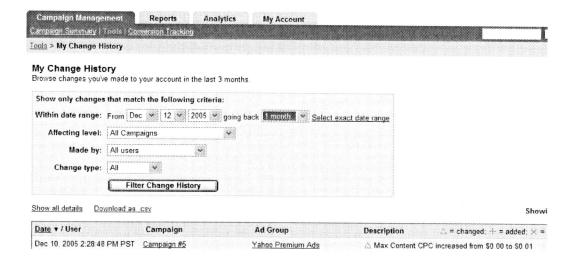

## XIII. Tools to Modify Your Campaigns

There are four main tools to manage your Campaigns and they can now be used on a global basis throughout your account.

| Campaign Management | Reports | Analytics | My Account |
|---|---|---|---|

Campaign Summary | Tools | Conversion Tracking

Do you have hundreds or even thousands of Ad Groups you are charged with managing? Now you can easily apply global changes without having to change each individual ad or Ad Group, which used to take hours.

---

### Four Tools to Modify Your Campaign

- ➢ Ad Text (Edit & Find)
- ➢ Copy or Move Keywords & Ad Text
- ➢ Keywords (Edit & Find)
- ➢ Find & Edit Max Cost-Per-Clicks

---

### NO STATISTIC TRANSFER ACROSS AD GROUPS

Keep in mind that when you move ads from one Ad Group to another the statistics for your keywords or ad text will *not* move with it. This is a big plus is you have poorly performing ads.

Use of these tools is backed by Google's powerful search technology and its filtering subset. You can search on keywords within ads, such as all those containing the term "Domain Names."

### A. Ad Text (Edit and Find)

Here you can easily change single ads or entire AdWords ads across your entire account. This includes the destination URLs of your ads.

**Find and Edit Ad Text**

Search > Select items > Review > Changes saved

Filter your Ad Groups, then apply ad text or URL changes all at once.

**1. FIND your ad text** (optional)
- Set filter(s) to narrow your search. The system will find ads that match all your filters.
- You may leave any filter blank. To find all ads in this account, simply skip this entire step.

**Look in these places:**

campaign name: [all campaigns ▼] [　　　　　　]

campaign status: [all ▼]

ad group name: [all ad groups ▼] [　　　　　　]

**..for ads that meet these criteria:**

text: ☑ Headline ☑ Display URL
☑ Description line 1 ☑ Destination URL
☑ Description line 2

[contains full word: ▼]

[　　　　　　　　　　　]

also search: ☐ Deleted ads
☐ Disapproved ads

**2. CHANGE or view ads that match my search filters** (Confirm or cancel in the next step)

○ * Replace [　　　　　　] with [　　　　　　]

○ * Change [headline ▼] to [　　　　　　]

## B. Copy or Move Keywords and Ad Text

With this tool you can easily copy or move various keywords and ad text to another Ad Group within your account.

| Campaign Management | Reports | Analytics | My Account |
|---|---|---|---|

Campaign Summary | Tools | Conversion Tracking

Tools > Copy/Move Keywords and Ad Text

### Copy/Move Keywords and Ad Text

Search ≫ Select items ≫ Set up destination ≫ Review ≫ Changes saved

Copy or move keywords and ad text to a single existing Ad Group or campaign. (Changes made through this tool won't require an editorial review.)

**1. Choose a search option.**

⊙ Search for keywords

○ Search for ad text

**2. Choose an action.**

⊙ Move -- Remove keywords/ad text from current location and add them to new location.

○ Copy -- Retain keywords/ad text in current location and add them to a new location.

Continue »

## C. Keywords (Edit and Find)

This is an obvious tool, but very powerful. With it you can change one or multiple keywords across your entire account, change keyword match types and change destination URLs.

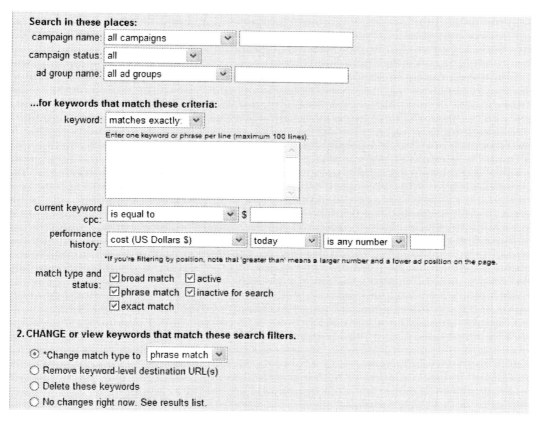

## SEARCH FOR BEST RANKING ADS

With the powerful tools to manage your campaign, you can even search on ads having a certain AdWords rank, those that are disabled, receive the most impressions, or those having a Click-Through-Rate above a certain percentage. Then use these tools to replicate ads that are working and for changing those that are not.

## D. Max Cost-Per-Click (Edit & Find)

Let's say you want to increase your maximum CPC by $0.10 for all keywords across your account. This is easily accomplished with this tool. You can also change every CPC within your account by a certain percentage.

**1. CHOOSE the type of Max CPC you want to find or change.**
- ⦿ Keyword-level Max CPCs (Find words by setting filters)
- ◯ Keyword-level Max CPCs (Enter a list of keywords and replacement Max CPCs)
- ◯ Ad Group Max CPCs (Change Max CPCs for entire Ad Groups)

**2. FIND keywords you'd like to change.** *(optional)*
- Set filter(s) to narrow your search. The system will find keywords that match all of your filters.
- You may leave any filter blank. To find *all* keywords in this account, simply skip this entire step.

**Search in these places:**

| | | |
|---|---|---|
| campaign name: | all campaigns ⌄ | |
| campaign status: | all ⌄ | |
| ad group name: | all ad groups ⌄ | |

**...for keywords that match these criteria:**

keyword:  matches exactly: ⌄

Enter one keyword or phrase per line (maximum 100 lines).

current keyword cpc:  is equal to ⌄  $

performance history:  cost (US Dollars $) ⌄   today ⌄   is any number ⌄

*If you're filtering by position, note that 'greater than' means a larger number and a lower ad position on the page.

match type and status:  ☑ broad match  ☑ active
☑ phrase match  ☑ inactive for search

## XIV. AdWord Reports

Under the "Reports" tab is a wealth of reporting options for your AdWords campaign.

Google provides seven detailed tracking reports that allow views of your advertising campaign from many different angles.

| Seven Adwords Reports |
| --- |
| 1. Keyword Report<br>2. Ad Text Report<br>3. Ad Image Report<br>4. URL Report<br>5. Account Report<br>6. Campaign Report<br>7. Ad Group Report |

Reports can be generated as frequently as daily, every Monday, or the first day of the month. These reports can then be easily set up to be emailed to you automatically in the format you desire.

### REPORT FORMATS

You may print your reports in .CSV, .XML, .HTML, and .TSV formats.

Below we will take a look at each of these reports and show you how they can help you best manage this feedback.

## A. Keyword Report

The fields from which you may choose to configure your Keyword Report are as follows:

| | | |
|---|---|---|
| | | Create Report |
| Report Type | Keyword Performance ⌄ | Learn more about report types |
| View | Summary ⌄ | |
| Date Range | ⊙ Last seven days ⌄ | |
| | ○ Dec ⌄ 27 ⌄ 2005 ⌄ - Jan ⌄ 2 ⌄ 2006 ⌄ | |
| Campaigns and Ad Groups | ⊙ All campaigns and ad groups | |
| | ○ Manually select from a list | |

**Advanced Options:**
**Columns**
Your report will display these columns:

| Campaign | Ad Group | Keyword | Keyword Matching | Keyword Status | Keyword Min CPC | Current Maximum CPC | Keyword Destination URL | Impressions | Clicks | CTR | Avg CPC | Cost | Avg Position |
|---|---|---|---|---|---|---|---|---|---|---|---|---|---|

▶ Add or Remove Columns

**Filters**
▶ Display only rows that match specific criteria

**Report Name**
Keyword Report                    ☐ Save this as a new report template

## USE FILTERS TO CUSTOMIZE REPORTS

You display only rows in your reports that match your specified criteria to customize your AdWords reports. Many times Google will provide too much information and it helps to filter some of it out.

## B. Ad Text Report

The fields from which you may choose to configure your Ad Text Report are:

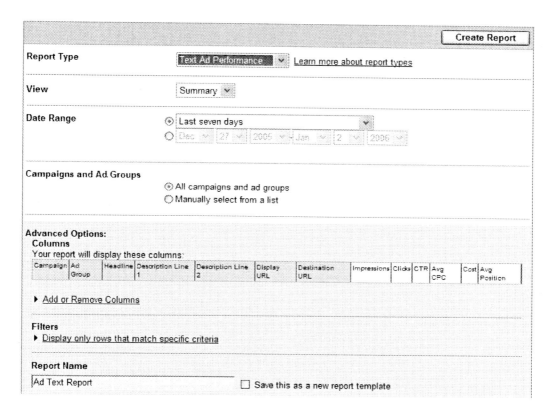

## LIMITED COST DATA IN AD TEXT REPORTS

You are unable to get key costing data in an Ad Text Report such as max/min CPC. Use the Keyword Report for this information.

### C. Image Ad Report

The fields from which you may choose to configure your Image Ad Report are:

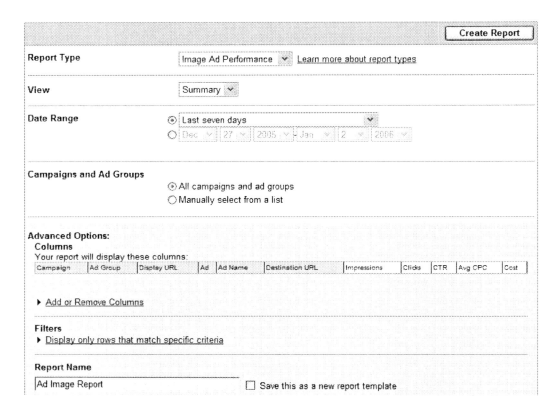

## NO SITE VISIBILITY IN IMAGE AD REPORTS

Since Image Ads are only shown across the Content Network, it would be helpful if you could generate a report on which sites resulted in clicks so that you could then use Site Targeting to hone where impressions of your Image Ads would be displayed.

## D. URL Report

The fields from which you may choose to configure your URL Report are as follows:

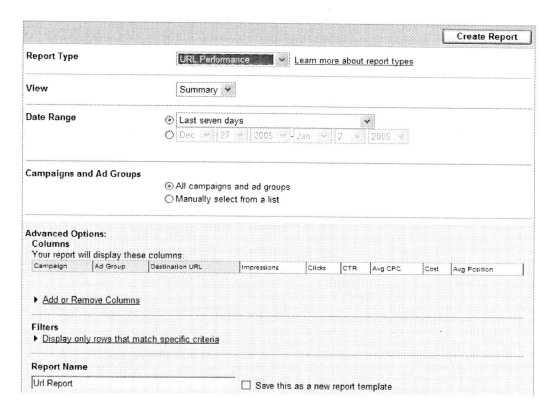

## LIMITED URL REPORT INFORMATION

The Ad Text and Keyword Reports provide everything that the URL Report does plus even more information. Do not waste time on this report if you are running one of the others.

### E. Account Report

The fields from which you may choose to configure your Account Report are as follows.

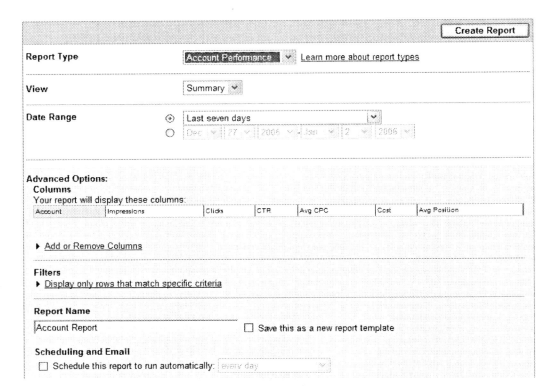

## THE BROAD ACCOUNT REPORT

> The Account Report is a broad-brush overview of your AdWords campaigns with much costing information. Do not use this report if you seek detailed click information.

## F. Campaign Report

The fields from which you may choose to configure your Campaign Report are:

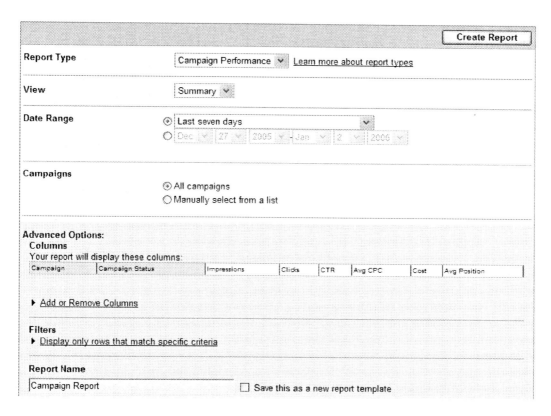

## REPORTS NOT REAL TIME

The above reporting is not in real time. There is a three hour buffer so that clicks within this window of time may not be reflected. Google updates campaign summary statistics on a more frequent basis than Ad Group and keyword statistics.

## G. Ad Group Report

The configure fields for your Ad Group Report are as follows:

## USE GOOGLE LINK TO MEASURE ADVERTISING SUCCESS

ROI is your best financial measurement of how well your Overture advertising campaign is proceeding, but there are other indicators like newsletter opt-ins and building brand identity. Another great measurement is the number of Websites that create links directly to your site. Google easily lets you monitor this by a simple command typed into the search box at Google.com:

| Google Search | Link:[Website].com |
|---|---|

The results shown will be all the Websites that have created a direct hyperlink to your Website. Monitor how the list grows as yet another indication of your Overture marketing success that may result in future sales even if you stop advertising!

## XV. My Account Options

There are a number of ways you can easily set your billing and user preferences for your AdWords account and we will discuss each below.

### A. Billing Summary

Under the Billing Summary tab you can generate reports on the frequency and amount Google has billed your account online or download as a .csv file.

| Campaign Management | Reports | Analytics | My Account |
|---|---|---|---|

Billing Summary | Billing Preferences | Access | User Preferences

**Billing Summary**

November 2005 - January 2006

Billing Summary is where you can print your financial receipts and invoices. Simply click on the invoice number for any line items to display the underlying invoice and print it. To print out receipts, select the "Payment Received" link for a particular payment from Google and select "Printable Receipt" to display in a printer-friendly format.

### B. Billing Preferences

Billing Preferences is where you specify the method in which Google bills you whether this be on a CPC basis or CPM basis.

| Campaign Management | Reports | Analytics | My Account |

Billing Summary | Billing Preferences | Access | User Preferences

**Billing Preferences**

This page is for viewing and managing your billing settings. If you're looking for the place where you revise your daily budget for a campaign, go to 'Campaign Management,' select the campaign, and click 'Edit Campaign Settings.'

**Billing and Payment [edit]**

Method of billing:    Post-pay Billing
Form of payment:    Credit Card

**Primary Payment Details [edit]**

## USE A REWARDS CREDIT CARD

Using a cash rebate/rewards or frequent flier credit card is a great way to receive perks from advertising on Google along with a possible tax deduction for this business expense! Google will automatically charge your card on a monthly basis and the transaction is paperless.

When setting up Billing Preferences you are asked the country in which you reside. If, for example, you have an EU billing address, Value Added Tax (VAT) will apply to your ad. Last, you must enter a credit or debit card (American Express, Visa, MasterCard, JCB, and debit cards having a MasterCard or Visa logo only). Google does not accept payment in any other form for your ad campaign.

## KEEP THOSE ADS SHOWING

Google allows you to place two credit cards on file in your AdWords account. One is used as a backup if your first credit card should become inactive due to expiration, etc. Your backup credit card will then be charged to keep your ads showing. Visit the "My Account" tab to input your second card.

## C. Access

Under the Access section you specify what users will have access to your AdWords account. You can invite new users via email. Google makes it simple to add multiple managers to your account.

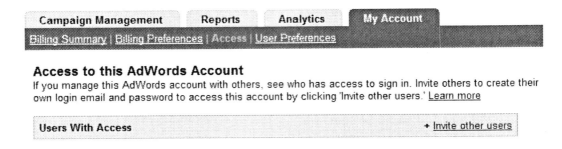

## USE ALERTS

Alerts is a free Google application that tracks keywords on Websites and automatically reports them to you by email. A great way to use this tool is to track your company name as Websites, blogs, etc use it. Google Alerts is a great way to track brand identity generated on Overture and when other Websites have reviewed your product or linked to your Website. Begin your Google Alert tracking today: www.Google.com/alerts?hl=en

There is a third party Website we like better than Google's own alert program. It is found at www.GoogleAlert.com and its basic service is also free. Some of the reasons we like it better are that multiple search results can be tracked. The results also give a *cashed* link that lets you jump right to the part of the Website referring to your product. Surprisingly, GoogleAlert.com also gives you more detailed results than Google itself and tells you the number of total results its tracking for the particular product name or term used.

### D. User Preferences

User Preferences allows you to specify such items as your login information, email preferences, and primary business type.

| Campaign Management | Reports | Analytics | My Account |
|---|---|---|---|

Billing Summary | Billing Preferences | Access | User Preferences

## User Preferences

Login Information  [edit in Google Accounts]

**Login Information [edit]**

| | |
|---|---|
| Email address: | John_Doe@[Website].com |
| Password: | ***** |
| Display language: | English (US) |

**Email Preferences [edit]**

| | |
|---|---|
| Newsletters: | Yes |
| Market research: | Yes |
| Special offers: | No, thanks |

**Primary Business Type [edit]**

| | |
|---|---|
| Business type: | LLC |

# KEEP THE HELP COMING

### GOOGLE GROUPS

Google has started an AdWords forum within Google Groups http://groups.google.com/ called "AdWords Help." It's a great place where advertisers help advertisers to maximize their AdWords campaigns.

### FREE INSIDE ADWORDS ASSISTANCE

Email the Inside AdWords Crew at:
inside-adwords@googlegroups.com with your tough AdWords questions.

### ADWORDS LEARNING CENTER

Google has created a great AdWords tutorial service that you can use. It's called the "Learning Center" and can be found the AdWords Help Center under the About AdWords section.

### SIGN UP WITH BOTTLETREEBOOKS.COM

Simply input your email address at:
www.bottletreebooks.com/GuerrillaGoogleAdvertising.htm to be notified when the next edition of "Guerrilla Google Advertising" will be released. Stay ahead of your competition.

BottleTreeBooks.com

**AdSense Unleashed**
**AdSense A-Z Plus 150 Killer Tips & Tricks**
Generate money quickly and easily as an AdSense publisher. Learn which ad units get the most clicks and where to put them on your Website. Also included is a huge list of the highest paying keyword groups in the United States, Australia, Canada, Ireland and the United Kingdom. Unlock the revenue potential of your Website today.
Buy the Book $15.98 | Buy the eBook $10.98
www.bottletreebooks.com/AdsenseUnleashed.htm

**Overture & Yahoo Advertising**
**Plus 110 Tips & Tricks for Getting the Most Clicks**
Get the tactics you need to make your Cost-Per-Click Yahoo advertising campaign a success. Learn how to get the most clicks at the lowest cost and how to get free $50 Yahoo advertising coupons. Beat your competition.
Buy the Book $14.98 | Buy the eBook $10.98
www.bottletreebooks.com/OvertureAdvertisingPages.htm

**Entire Tales & Poems of Edgar Allan Poe**
**Photographic & Annotated Edition**
This book brings Poe to life as never before. It contains a great foreword by Andrew Barger and includes his annotations, word definitions, foreign language translations, and background information about Poe's stories and poems that provide insight into

their underlying meaning. Photographs of Poe's many loves and the literary figures he satired in his stories are provided. Poems sent to Poe by his many romantic interests and his poems in response are set forth. Also included are five little-known Poe tales: "[The Bloodhounds]," "Cabs," "Morning on the Wissahiccon," "[The Rats of Park Theatre]," "Some Secrets of the Magazine Prison House," and "The Swiss Bell-Ringers." Read the works of America's most brilliant and mysterious author as you never have before.

Buy the Book | Buy the eBook $10.98
www.bottletreebooks.com/EntireTales.htm

### Coffee with Poe

This is a historical novel that retells Edgar Allan Poe's life in only the way Andrew Barger can. The novel is filled with actual letters to his three fiancées, his literary contemporaries (Longfellow, Irving, and Hawthorne), and his bitter enemies. Read about Poe's constant struggles with poverty, love, and acceptance by the literary community. Have a cup of *Coffee with Poe* and live his life as never presented.

Buy the Book $10.98 | Buy the eBook $5.98
www.bottletreebooks.com/CoffeewithPoePages.htm

BottleTreeBooks.com

Signup for our free mailing list by sending a blank email to:
newsletter@bottletreebooks.com

Include the subject heading: **Newsletter**

Printed in the United Kingdom
by Lightning Source UK Ltd.
113910UKS00002B/3-4